Teacher's Pack

# ICT InteraCT
## for KS3

Teacher's Pack **2**

# ICT InteraCT

## for KS3

### Bob Reeves

Consultant: Alan Plumpton

**HODDER**
EDUCATION
AN HACHETTE UK COMPANY

The Publishers would like to thank the following for permission to reproduce copyright material:
**Photo credits: 5.1 Written Task answers** www.sokei.fr; **5.2 End of Unit Activity** Stephen Kelly/PA Archive/PA Photos; **5.3. End of Unit Activity** Stockbyte/Getty Images; **7.1. New paddling pool information** and **Controlling the self-service kiosk** © Argos Limited 2007; **Module 5 assignment** © Rosemary Roberts/Alamy.

Every effort has been made to trace all copyright holders, but if any have been inadvertently overlooked the Publishers will be pleased to make the necessary arrangements at the first opportunity.

Although every effort has been made to ensure that website addresses are correct at time of going to press, Hodder Education cannot be held responsible for the content of any website mentioned in this book. It is sometimes possible to find a relocated web page by typing in the address of the home page for a website in the URL window of your browser.

Hachette's policy is to use papers that are natural, renewable and recyclable products and made from wood grown in sustainable forests. The logging and manufacturing processes are expected to conform to the environmental regulations of the country of origin.

Orders: please contact Bookpoint Ltd, 130 Milton Park, Abingdon, Oxon OX14 4SB. Telephone: +44 (0)1235 827720. Fax: +44 (0)1235 400454. Lines are open 9.00–5.00, Monday to Saturday, with a 24-hour message answering service. Visit our website at www.hoddereducation.co.uk

© Bob Reeves 2008
First published in 2008
by Hodder Education
an Hachette UK Company
Carmelite House
50 Victoria Embankment
London EC4Y 0DZ

Impression number        9
Year                     2018

Cover photo Jupiter images/Corbis
Typeset in ITC Officina Sans 11pt/14pt by Pantek Arts Ltd, Maidstone, Kent
Printed in Great Britain by Hobbs The Printers, Totton, Hants

A catalogue record for this title is available from the British Library

ISBN: 978 0340 94101 0

# CONTENTS

# Introduction

Welcome to ICT InteraCT 2. The course is made up of six main modules, each of which contains a number of units. In addition, Module 7 contains three Integrated Tasks to be completed once pupils have worked through the rest of the course. There is a range of resources in each module and unit. Pupils can access these resources by clicking on the appropriate icon on the Dynamic Learning page.

**Whole Class Presentations:** These are PowerPoint presentations that introduce each unit.

**Starter Activities:** These are quick tasks to help pupils get started with the topic.

**Case Studies:** These are animated presentations that introduce each module. They contain questions and the presentation can be stopped at any time for class discussions.

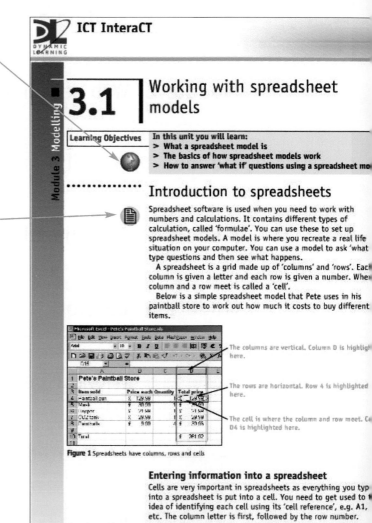

**Written Tasks:** These are tasks that do not require the use of a computer. They can be used in class, or as homework.

**Practical Tasks:** These are tasks that need to be completed on the computer.

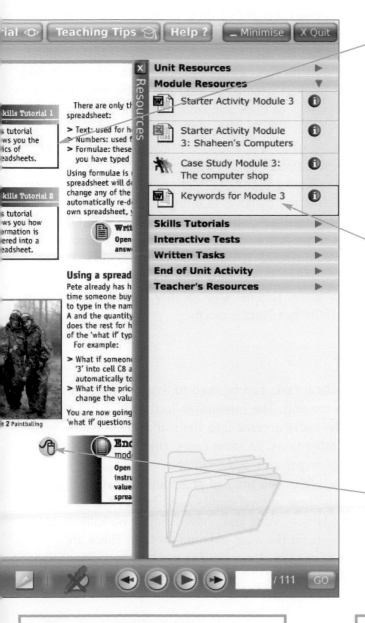

**Unit Resources** ▶
**Module Resources** ▼
📄 Starter Activity Module 3 ⓘ
📄 Starter Activity Module 3: Shaheen's Computers ⓘ
👥 Case Study Module 3: The computer shop ⓘ
📄 Keywords for Module 3 ⓘ
**Skills Tutorials** ▶
**Interactive Tests** ▶
**Written Tasks** ▶
**End of Unit Activity** ▶
**Teacher's Resources** ▶

/ 111  GO

 **Skills Tutorials:** These contain instructions on how to carry out certain tasks on the computer. There are two versions of these:

> a Word version that can be printed (available in Office 2000, 2003 and 2007)
> an animated version.

**Keywords:** These list all of the new words for each module.

 **Interactive Tests:** These are online tests that are marked automatically, and mainly used to test knowledge.

  **End of Unit Activities:** These are levelled activities taken at the end of each unit.

  **End of Module Assignments:** These are levelled activities for pupils to take at the end of each module.

ICT InteraCT for KS3 2

# Teacher's Guidance

The course is designed to cover all aspects of the Programme of Study and the Teaching Objectives for Year 8.

There is comprehensive Teacher's Guidance for all module and unit activities. This includes: Lesson objectives, Programme of Study and Framework references, cross-references to the Sample Teaching Units, a resource listing, an outline lesson plan, guidance on levelling, keywords and cross-references to Every Child Matters (ECM) and Personal Learning and Thinking Skills (PLTS).

In terms of ECM, ICT mainly provides opportunities for pupils to 'enjoy and achieve' and 'achieve economic well-being'. Some units allow pupils to 'stay safe'.

In terms of PLTS, ICT mainly provides opportunities for pupils to become 'independent enquirers', 'reflective learners' and 'creative thinkers'. Some units allow other PLTS criteria to be met. Any work done in pairs or groups will allow pupils to demonstrate 'team worker' skills.

There are opportunities for pupils to work collaboratively throughout, and teachers should exercise their own judgement as to whether to take these opportunities. Teachers need to balance the requirement for pupils to generate evidence of their own work, with the benefits of collaborative work.

In addition, there are generic self and peer review documents that can be used with most tasks. These can be found at the back of this pack, as well as in the 'Global Resources' section in the resources folder of the Network version of the Dynamic Learning CD-ROM. Reviewing others' work and taking feedback into account are both important skills for ICT and will help to provide evidence of higher levels. There are also three Integrated Tasks in Module 7, which encourage pupils to work across a range of ICT strands. Pupils should be encouraged to create portfolios of work for these. This helps to identify higher level pupils as developing an e-portfolio is a feature of L6.

# Assessment

The Written and Practical Tasks can be used to assess progress as the pupil works through the unit. The Interactive Tests are marked automatically and the marks entered into the markbook. Answer sheets are provided for all other tasks. In some cases, these are *suggested* answers as a range of responses may be suitable.

The End of Unit Activities and the End of Module Assignments are levelled. Full advice on how to level pupils' work is provided in the Teacher's Notes. In addition, most tasks have levelled worksheets so that you can give the pupil the most appropriate task. These are levelled as L3/4, L4/5 or L5/6. The following symbols have been used to differentiate the levels:

■   Levels 3/4

●   Levels 4/5

▲   Levels 5/6

# The Markbook

The *ICT InteraCT Dynamic Learning Network Edition CD-ROM 2* features an interactive assessment engine and markbook. As pupils complete the short interactive tests featured throughout the Dynamic Learning resource, their scores are recorded in the markbook area. These tests are designed to test knowledge and understanding, and have marks/feedback associated with them.

Both the scores achieved by pupils and the associated feedback for each test can be fed into reports at the click of a button. The information can also be exported from the assessment engine in the form of a .csv file, which in turn allows schools to input the data into their chosen information system.

In addition to the automatically marked interactive tests, there is a facility that allows teachers to allocate levels to the End of Unit Activities and End of Module Assignments. These activities are designed to assess pupils' capability in relation to different skills and strands of ICT, and are levelled at L3-4, L4-5 or L5/6 (with additional opportunities for extension work). The accompanying Teacher's Notes provide guidance for every levelled activity, specifying for the teacher how to assess work completed by pupils to particular levels. The automated markbook allows teachers to allocate levels to pupils/the activities they've completed. All of the activities/levels are mapped to the revised Level Descriptions. These data then feed into the report facility, allowing teachers to generate reports quickly and easily, either alongside or in isolation of the information fed in as pupils complete the interactive activities noted above.

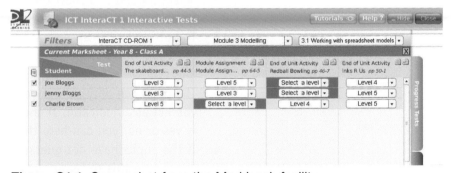

**Figure S1.1** Screenshot from the Markbook facility

# Software used

The resources on the Dynamic Learning CD-ROM reference Microsoft Office 2000 or later versions.

# Links to the *ICT for KS3 Activity and Assessment CD-ROM*

The activities on the CD-ROM have been linked to the *ICT for Key Stage 3 Activity and Assessment CD-ROM*, which is available separately from Hodder Education. This provides a bank of differentiated, scenario-based tasks matched to L3-6 of the Level Descriptions (with opportunities for extension by virtue of the Integrated Tasks). Please note that it is not necessary for purchasers of *ICT InteraCT* to use the content of this CD-ROM in order to use the course, but the activities included on it do provide teachers and pupils with additional opportunities to test knowledge, skills and capabilities to the Level Descriptions.

# Quick Starters

The Starter Activities described here can be used in addition or as an alternative to the full Starter Activities that can be found on the Dynamic Learning CD-ROM. They are designed only to last for a few minutes.

The exercises are based around the Keywords in each module. The exercises can be used to introduce and/or reinforce the keywords as you work through each unit in each module. They can also be used as a prompt for further discussion.

Keywords labels for each module are provided separately. These can be printed and used separately, or used as part of these exercises.

A separate glossary of keywords is also provided at the back of the Pupil's Book.

## 20 questions

### Preparation

Print the Keywords label sheet for the module you are working on.

### Doing the activity

1 Select a pupil and show them one keyword. Other pupils should not be able to see the keyword you have given them.
2 The other pupils can now ask the pupil 20 questions to try and find out what the keyword is. A guess at the keyword counts as a question.
3 The pupil can only answer yes or no to the questions. As teacher you act as adjudicator. If the pupil is not sure whether the answer is yes or no, you can help them.
4 If the pupils have not guessed after 20 questions, they lose. You can reduce this to fewer questions if you prefer.

## Just a minute

### Preparation

Print the Keywords label sheet for the module you are working on.

### Doing the activity

1 Select a pupil and show them one keyword. The other pupils should also be told the keyword.
2 The selected pupil now has to talk about the keyword for one minute, without deviation, hesitation or repetition.
3 If they deviate, hesitate or repeat themselves, other pupils can 'challenge' them by putting their hands up and explaining which of the three errors they made.
4 If it is a fair challenge, the remaining time passes to the pupil who made the challenge.

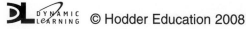

5   The winner is whoever is still talking when the minute is up.
6   You act as judge and timekeeper.

# Draw It

## Preparation

Print the Keywords label sheet for the module you are working on.

## Doing the activity

1   Give one pupil a keyword that the other pupils do not see.
2   The pupil then has one minute to get the other pupils to guess what the keyword is, but only by drawing (which they can do on the whiteboard).
3   The other pupils put up their hands and guess what the keyword is. The pupil who gets it right then gets to do the next keyword.
4   If no one guesses correctly after one minute, select another pupil to try and draw the same or a new keyword.
5   You act as timekeeper.

This can also be adapted as a smaller group exercise, with one person drawing for others in their group.

# What's the question?

## Preparation

Print the Keywords label sheet for the module you are working on.

## Doing the activity

1   Read out a keyword (the answer).
2   Pupils have to ask a question that would lead to this answer being given. For example, if the keyword is 'Bias', the question might be: "What should you check for when you read information on a website?", or if the keyword is "Bold", the question might be: "How can you make a title stand out in a document?"

This can also be adapted as a small group exercise or pairs activity.

# Starter Activities

## Resources needed

1    Starter Activity worksheet*
2    Starter Activity answers document

*One provided for every module

1–3 hours

## How to use the resources

All of the tasks on the CD-ROM will help pupils to develop their problem-solving skills as well as their ICT capability. These Starter Activities focus specifically on developing problem-solving skills and are designed to make pupils more aware of problem-solving techniques, which they can then apply.

There is one Starter Activity for each module. You may ask pupils to complete all of the questions on the worksheets, or you pick out individual questions to cover particular aspects of problem-solving.

The guidance given here is generic to all modules. There are also answer sheets for each activity. The Starter Activities are **not** designed to elicit a National Curriculum level, but to get the pupils thinking about problem-solving in relation to ICT.

## Problem-solving skills

Problem-solving is defined by the QCA as follows:

"where there is a need to bridge a gap between a current situation and a desired one".

A common interpretation of this is that a pupil is able to apply existing skills and knowledge in order to identify and implement effective solutions to new problems.

There are four main stages of problem-solving:

1    Identify and understand the problem.
2    Plan ways to solve the problem and identify the most appropriate solution.
3    Monitor progress.
4    Review the solution.

Problem-solving skills include the ability to:

>    think creatively in order to solve a problem
>    evaluate alternative solutions and choose the most appropriate
>    manage and retrieve information related to the problem
>    keep track of progress and check results
>    communicate effectively to the target audience/user
>    take account of feedback from the target audience/user or from peer review
>    make and develop hypotheses.

# Problem-solving techniques

There are many techniques that can be used to encourage the development of problem-solving skills. The advice given here is not designed to be exhaustive, but does suggest techniques that could be used with these Starter Activities and the main tasks on the CD-ROM.

Some of these techniques are useful for generating ideas, while others are more useful as planning tools and others for reviewing the solution.

These exercises lend themselves to pair or small group work as collaborative working is a key aspect of problem-solving. Many of the techniques listed here require group work.

## Generating ideas

### Brainstorming

This is a method for generating ideas. In small groups, elect one pupil as the chairperson and scribe. Pupils should be encouraged to come up with as many ideas as they possibly can. All ideas should be written down. Ideas are likely to flow in a fairly random manner, but this is to be expected and none of the ideas should be discounted at this stage. Pupils should be encouraged to think outside of any constraints, such as time, money or resources.

### In others' shoes

This is a method for seeing a problem from someone else's point of view. For example, if you were asked to design a website for a company, it might be useful to put yourself in the customer's shoes. This method works well in a group where pupils work independently at first and then combine their ideas later.

### Spider diagrams

This is a method of generating ideas and linking them together in a diagrammatic form. The main problem is written in the centre and then all of the factors branch off from this. Factors can be grouped together into sub-problems. Software is available to allow this to be done electronically. Figure S1.1 shows a simple spider diagram where the problem is whether the school should upgrade its computer suite.

**Figure S1.1**

## Planning

### Flowcharts

These are particularly useful where all of the actions required to solve a problem have been identified. The flowchart can then be used to put the information into a sequence. Although the exact shape of the symbols is not that important as this stage, it is useful to identify actions and decisions, with different routes coming from decision boxes. Figure S1.2 shows a simple flowchart that shows the processes for putting together a questionnaire in order to get the information needed to draw a conclusion.

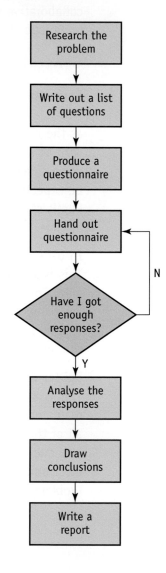

**Figure S1.2**

### Decision trees

This technique is particularly useful where there are different paths that could be taken. It is a visual way of working through the consequences of each course of action. At each point, a decision is made, which leads to a further decision. Figure S1.3 shows a decision tree for deciding on whether to upgrade the computer suite in a school.

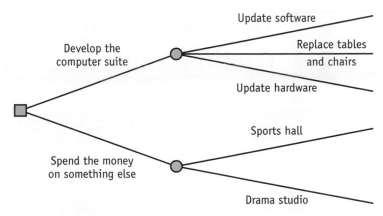

**Figure S1.3**

### Gantt charts

These are similar to a timeline and can be used as a planning tool. Once all of the steps required to solve a problem are known, they can be put into a Gantt chart. There will be dependencies in the steps. For example, if you were designing a website, you would need to decide on which software to use before you could start creating it. The Gantt chart shows these dependencies. Figure S1.4 shows a Gantt chart for carrying out questionnaire-based research in order to solve a problem.

| ID | Task Name | Start | Finish | Duration | Aug 2006 | | | | | | | | | | |
|----|-----------|-------|--------|----------|----|----|----|----|----|----|----|----|----|----|----|
| | | | | | 21 | 22 | 23 | 24 | 25 | 26 | 27 | 28 | 29 | 30 | 31 |
| 1 | Research the problem | 22/08/2006 | 22/08/2006 | 1d | ■ | | | | | | | | | | |
| 2 | Write out a list of questions | 23/08/2006 | 23/08/2006 | 1d | | ■ | | | | | | | | | |
| 3 | Produce a questionnaire | 24/08/2006 | 24/08/2006 | 1d | | | ■ | | | | | | | | |
| 4 | Hand out the questionnaire | 25/08/2006 | 25/08/2006 | 1d | | | | ■ | | | | | | | |
| 5 | Check you have enough responses | 28/08/2006 | 28/08/2006 | 1d | | | | | | | | ■ | | | |
| 6 | Analyse responses | 28/08/2006 | 28/08/2006 | 1d | | | | | | | | ■ | | | |
| 7 | Draw conclusions | 28/08/2006 | 28/08/2006 | 1d | | | | | | | | ■ | | | |
| 8 | Write a report | 29/08/2006 | 29/08/2006 | 1d | | | | | | | | | ■ | | |

**Figure S1.4**

## Reviewing

### Strengths/weaknesses

When a solution is complete, the strengths and weaknesses of the solution can be analysed. This involves testing how well the solution solves the problems. This may be done in comparison with a list of objectives that would need to be defined in the earlier stages.

# 1 Teacher's Notes
## Finding and presenting information

## Module structure

This module on finding and presenting information builds on Module 1 of the Interact 1 course. There is a greater emphasis on considering where information comes from and checking its validity. The module moves on to look at the different ways in which information can be presented.

1.1 Evaluating information found on websites
1.2 Checking the validity of information
1.3 Choosing a search engine
1.4 Presenting information using a slideshow
1.5 Presenting information using audio

Unit 1.1 starts with pupils evaluating information found on websites. This is developed further in Unit 1.2. Unit 1.3 focuses specifically on choosing which search engine to use and understanding more about how they work. Unit 1.4 looks at the creation of non-linear presentations and Unit 1.5 focuses on the use of audio presentations, asking pupils to create a radio report. As with all the modules, there are some module resources that you can use before you start on the units:

> Module 1 Case Study
> Module 1 Starter Activities

## Assessment

All assessments in this module are designed to allow pupils to demonstrate L4–6. There are levelled activities and interpretation of the levels is provided in the Teacher's Notes for each unit.

There is also a levelled Module Assignment that pupils can work on when all the units are complete. This is designed to cover all aspects of this module. This is a differentiated activity and you should give each pupil the worksheet that is most appropriate to the level they are working towards. The interpretation of levels for the Module Assignment is given below.

## Assessment guidance for Module Assignment

**L4** Pupils understand the need for care in framing questions when collecting, finding and interrogating information. They interpret their findings, question plausibility and recognise that poor-quality information leads to unreliable results. They add to, amend and combine different forms of information from a variety of sources. They use ICT to present information in different forms and show they are aware of the intended audience and the need for quality in their presentations.

Pupils should collect information from one source and, although they may not check the validity of the information, they should not include any information that is clearly implausible.

They may need some guidance in selecting the most appropriate way to create the presentation, but will work largely unaided in putting a presentation together. They should show an awareness of at least one of the two audiences although they may find it difficult to appeal to both with the same presentation.

**L5** Pupils select the information they need for different purposes, check and organise it in a form suitable for processing. They use ICT to structure,

refine and present information in different forms and styles for specific purposes and audiences.

Pupils collect information from more than one source and only include what they know to be accurate. Pupils need no guidance in choosing the most appropriate way to present the information and can appeal to both adults and children, perhaps by creating a non-linear presentation with some parts aimed at the adults and some parts aimed at the children. They can complete the table to explain what they have done.

**L6** Pupils plan and design ICT-based solutions to meet a specific purpose and audience, demonstrating increased integration and efficiency in their use of ICT tools. They develop and refine their work to enhance its quality, using a greater range and complexity of information. Where necessary, they use complex lines of enquiry to test hypotheses. They present their ideas in a variety of ways and show a clear sense of audience.

Pupils can work largely unaided on the presentation using information from a range of sources. They can appeal to both the older and younger audience and complete the table to explain what they have done. The key discriminator of L6 pupils is their ability to empathise with an unfamiliar audience (the visually impaired) and make changes that are suitable. They may carry out research to find what features they could add with this audience in mind, such as increased use of sound, larger font sizes and contrasting foreground and background colours.

# Suggested answers to questions posed in the Case Study

Q What information might people want to know? Where can Arthur get the information from? How can he be sure that the information is reliable and accurate?

**Suggested answers:**
Visitors to the park might want information about:

> the local area – what the sites of interest are, where they are, some history about them
> local attractions – where they are, how to get there, when they open, how much they cost
> local facilities – shops, restaurants, hotels, leisure centres, cinemas, etc.

Arthur can get the information:

> direct from the local organisations
> from websites
> by talking to the local people.

Arthur can ensure reliability and accuracy by:

> checking the information from more than one source
> thinking about the purpose for which he is given the information, e.g. a hotel is trying to attract customers so their information may be biased
> checking the information is up to date.

Q What search engine could Arthur use? Why would he use one search engine rather than another?

**Suggested answers:**
Arthur could use Google, Ask Jeeves (Kids), AltaVista, Yahoo, Metacrawler, etc. His choice of search engine could be based on the coverage of the Internet or on popularity, e.g. most people use Google because it has become the most popular. Some search engines, such as Ask Jeeves and Yahoo, have categories within which you can search, which can be quicker. Ask Jeeves (Kids) allows the user to type in questions rather than keywords, which younger pupils might find helpful.

Q Can Arthur trust the information that is on the Paulin Hotel website? Why might the information on the hotel website be biased? Is the information on the website based on fact or opinion?

**Suggested answers:**
Arthur should be sceptical about the information on the Paulin Hotel website. Their purpose is to persuade people to go to the hotel so statements such as "Our leisure facilities are the best in the area" may be biased. Arthur would need to check this information either by visiting the hotel himself or by checking other hotel facilities to see if they are better.

Q In what different ways could Arthur present the information to the tourists?

**Suggested answers:**
> Printed material, e.g. a word-processed report or a desktop published article.
> Multimedia slideshow.
> Sound recording (for example, a podcast).
> Video.

Q What problems might there be with the way that Arthur has set up the slideshow? How could he make the slideshow more suitable for the audience?

**Suggested answers:**
The problems are that:

> viewers have to watch every slide even if they are not interested in it
> they have to wait to get to the slide on the bit they are interested in
> if they start viewing part way through the presentation, they have to wait until it loops and starts all over again.

Arthur should:

> set up a menu slide where viewers can select which parts of the presentation they want to look at
> allow viewers to start and stop the presentation at any time and move forward and back through the slides in any order.

Q What different types of information do the visitors need? What is the best way of providing this information in each case?

**Suggested answers:**
The point here is that the way the information is presented is suited to the information needs of the visitor.

> Visitors may want a map that gives directions for a local walk. This should be presented in a format that allows them to take it with them on the walk.
> Visitors may want information on the local hotels. A 'virtual tour' of the hotels might be useful so they can compare hotels without having to visit them.
> Visitors who are visually impaired may need an audio version of the slideshow.

# 1.1 Teacher's Notes
## Evaluating information found on websites

## Lesson objectives

This is the first unit of two on techniques for evaluating information found on websites. It builds on the work that was done in Unit 2.3 of the InteraCT 1 course, focusing on ways that pupils can form judgements about the reliability of information found on the web.

Pupils consider what a URL can tell them about the source of the information and then go on to think about the purpose of the different types of organisations that put information on the Internet.

Pupils learn that some sites are well-known and on that basis may be trustworthy, whereas other sites are completely unknown. They are asked to make judgements about what is fact and what is opinion.

## PoS reference

2.1a) consider systematically the information needed to solve a problem, complete a task or answer a question, and explore how it will be used.

2.1b) use and refine search methods to obtain information that is well matched to purpose, by selecting appropriate sources.

2.1c) collect and enter quantitative and qualitative information, checking its accuracy.

2.1d) analyse and evaluate information, judging its value, accuracy, plausibility and bias.

2.4a) review, modify and evaluate work as it progresses, reflecting critically and using feedback.

2.4b) reflect on their own and others' uses of ICT to help them develop and improve their ideas and the quality of their work.

2.4c) reflect on what they have learnt and use these insights to improve future work.

3a) use a range of information, with different characteristics, structures and purposes, and evaluation of how it matches requirements and its fitness for purpose.

3b) use a variety of information sources, including large data sets, in a range of contexts.

## Framework reference

Finding things out:

> Using data and information sources: understand how the content and style of an information source affect its suitability for particular purposes; evaluate how well an information source supports a task; justify the use of an information source

## STU reference

8.3

## A&A CD-ROM reference

Strand DTP Activities 1–4
**InteraCT 1 Ref:** Unit 2.3

## PLTS

Independent enquirer
Reflective learner

## Every Child Matters

Enjoy and achieve
Achieve economic well-being

## Differentiation and inclusion

Levelled worksheets in the Unit
Assessment
Opportunities for group work

## Keywords

> Fact
> Opinion
> Reliable
> URL

# Resources required

**Whole Class Presentation: Unit 1.1**

**Written Task: Trusting websites**

**End of Unit Activity 1.1: Evaluating information (L4/5)**
**End of Unit Activity 1.1: Evaluating information (L5/6)**
**End of Unit Activity 1.1: Evaluating information (Suggested answers)**

**Interactive Test: Information on the Internet**

**Pages 8–9 of the Pupil's Book**

# Teaching notes

1  Use the Module 1 Case Study to introduce pupils to the ways that information can be presented.
2  Use the Whole Class Presentation to explain the objectives of this unit and provide an overview.
3  Ask pupils to look at pages 8 to 9 of the Pupil's Book. This can be projected if facilities exist.
4  Explain how you can use parts of the URL to identify the type of person or organisation behind the website. Ask pupils for examples. Ask the pupils for any other codes that they have come across that are not listed in the book.
5  Pupils complete the Interactive Test.
6  Explain to pupils that different types of organisations have different purposes in putting information on their websites. In many cases, this is to sell things.
7  Pupils complete the Written Task, 'Trusting websites'.
8  Explain the difference between a fact and an opinion. Mention that facts can be disputed.
9  Pupils complete the End of Unit Activity, 'Evaluating information'.

# Assessment guidance for End of Unit Activity

**L4** Pupils understand the need for care in framing questions when collecting, finding and interrogating information. They interpret their findings, question plausibility and recognise that poor-quality information leads to unreliable results. They add to, amend and combine different forms of information from a variety of sources.

Pupils support their answers with information from one other source. They should not include any information that is clearly implausible although at this level you would not expect them to double check the information with a further source. They copy and paste information from the websites into the document, although they may not summarise or synthesise this information in any way.

**L5** Pupils select the information they need for different purposes, check its accuracy and organise it in a form suitable for processing.

Pupils support their answers with information from at least one source in most cases. They may not be able to fully justify their answers with information from more than one website in every case. They should attempt to summarise the information, copying and pasting relevant information from the websites into their own document. Sources should be quoted.

**L6** Pupils develop and refine their work to enhance its quality, using a greater range and complexity of information. Where necessary, they use complex lines of enquiry to test hypotheses.

At this level, pupils should be backing up their answers with information from at least two different sources. The information should support their answers and should be from sites that appear to be reliable. The key characteristic at this level is that several sources of information are used. Sources should be quoted with some indication of why pupils trust this particular source.

# 1.2 | Teacher's Notes
## Checking the validity of information

## Lesson objectives

This is the second of two units on techniques for evaluating information found on websites. It builds on the work done in Unit 1.1 which in turn develops the work that pupils did in InteraCT 1. The focus of this unit is on checking the validity of information building on the theme of checking facts introduced in Unit 1.1. Pupils consider sites listed as the result of a web search and look at the source of the information and links to and from the sites.

Pupils also consider bias and why some information may be presented in a biased way. Finally, pupils consider how up-to-date information is and whether it is valid if the information is old.

## PoS reference

2.1a) consider systematically the information needed to solve a problem, complete a task or answer a question, and explore how it will be used.

2.1b) use and refine search methods to obtain information that is well matched to purpose, by selecting appropriate sources.

2.1c) collect and enter quantitative and qualitative information, checking its accuracy.

2.1d) analyse and evaluate information, judging its value, accuracy, plausibility and bias.

2.4a) review, modify and evaluate work as it progresses, reflecting critically and using feedback.

2.4b) reflect on their own and others' uses of ICT to help them develop and improve their ideas and the quality of their work.

2.4c) reflect on what they have learnt and use these insights to improve future work.

3a) use a range of information, with different characteristics, structures and purposes, and evaluation of how it matches requirements and its fitness for purpose.

3b) use a variety of information sources, including large data sets, in a range of contexts.

## Framework reference

Finding things out:

> Using data and information sources: understand how the content and style of an information source affect its suitability for particular purposes; evaluate how well an information source supports a task; justify the use of an information source

## STU reference

8.3

## A&A CD-ROM reference

Strand DTP Activities 1–4
**InteraCT 1 Ref:** Unit 2.3

## PLTS

Independent enquirer
Reflective learner

## Every Child Matters

Enjoy and achieve
Achieve economic well-being

## Differentiation and inclusion

Levelled worksheets in the Unit
Assessment
Opportunities for group work

## Keywords

> Bias
> Up-to-date
> Validity

# Resources required

 **Whole Class Presentation: Unit 1.2**

 **Written Task: Checking validity**
**Written Task: Checking validity (Suggested answers)**

 **End of Unit Activity 1.2: Football or fishing – you decide (L4-5)**
**End of Unit Activity 1.2: Football or fishing – you decide (L5-6)**

 **Interactive Test: Biased information**

**Pages 10–13 of the Pupil's Book**

# Teaching notes

1 Use the Module 1 Case Study to introduce pupils to the ways that information can be presented.
2 Use the Whole Class Presentation to explain the objectives of this unit and provide an overview.
3 Ask pupils to look at pages 10 to 13 of the Pupil's Book. This can be projected if facilities exist.
4 Explain to pupils how they might come across 'facts' that contradict each other and explain how they can use information from websites to check facts.
5 Pupils complete the Written Task 'Checking validity'.
6 Explain the concept of bias and the reasons that it may exist in information, e.g. people have particular points of view or perhaps they present things in the best possible light.
7 Pupils complete the Interactive Test.
8 Discuss the concept of how information can become out of date.
9 Pupils complete the End of Unit Activity 'Football or fishing – you decide'.

# Assessment guidance for End of Unit Activity

**L4** Pupils combine and refine different forms of information from various sources. Pupils understand the need for care in framing questions when collecting, finding and interrogating information. They interpret their findings, question plausibility and recognise that poor-quality information leads to unreliable results.

Pupils support their conclusion with information from one source. They should not include any information that is clearly implausible although at this level you would not expect them to double check the information with a further source. They copy and paste information from the websites into the document, although they may not summarise or synthesise this information in any way.

**L5** Pupils select the information they need for different purposes, check its accuracy and organise it in a form suitable for processing. They use ICT to structure, refine and present information in different forms and styles for specific purposes and audiences.

Pupils support their conclusion with information from more than one source. They may not be able to fully justify their answers with information from more than one website in every case. They should attempt to summarise the information, copying and pasting relevant information from the websites into their own document. Sources should be quoted.

**L6** Pupils develop and refine their work to enhance its quality, using a greater range and complexity of information. Where necessary, they use complex lines of enquiry to test hypotheses.

At this level, pupils should be backing up their conclusion with information from at least two sources. The information should support their conclusion and should be from sites that appear to be reliable. The key characteristic is that several sources of information are used. Sources should be quoted, with some indication of why they trust this particular source.

# 1.3 Teacher's Notes
## Choosing a search engine

## Lesson objectives

This unit focuses on the way that search engines work and why you might choose one search engine over another. Pupils are asked to think about a search engine that they use and to research other search engines that are available. They look at the features offered by different search engines, e.g. some are specifically for children, some use several other search engines. The basic methodology behind how search engines work is explained, including the way that links are used to decide how to rank the results of a search.

This unit builds directly on the work that pupils did in Units 2.1 and 2.2 of the InteraCT 1 course.

## PoS reference

2.1a) consider systematically the information needed to solve a problem, complete a task or answer a question, and explore how it will be used.

2.1b) use and refine search methods to obtain information that is well matched to purpose, by selecting appropriate sources.

2.1c) collect and enter quantitative and qualitative information, checking its accuracy.

2.1d) analyse and evaluate information, judging its value, accuracy, plausibility and bias.

2.2b) solve problems by developing, exploring and structuring information, and deriving new information for a particular purpose.

2.3a) use a range of ICT tools to present information in forms that are fit for purpose, meet audience needs and suit the content.

2.3b) communicate and exchange information (including digital communication) effectively, safely and responsibly.

2.3c) use technical terms appropriately and correctly.

2.4a) review, modify and evaluate work as it progresses, reflecting critically and using feedback.

2.4b) reflect on their own and others' uses of ICT to help them develop and improve their ideas and the quality of their work.

2.4c) reflect on what they have learnt and use these insights to improve future work.

3a) use a range of information, with different characteristics, structures and purposes, and evaluation of how it matches requirements and its fitness for purpose.

3b) use a variety of information sources, including large data sets, in a range of contexts.

3c) use and review of the effectiveness of different ICT tools, including a range of software applications, in terms of meeting user needs and solving problems.

## STU reference

8.3

## A&A CD-ROM reference

Strand DTP Activities 1–4
**InteraCT 1 Ref:** Units 2.1 and 2.2

## PLTS

Independent enquirer
Reflective learner

## Every Child Matters

Enjoy and achieve
Achieve economic well-being

## Differentiation and inclusion

Opportunities for group work

## Keywords

> Hits
> Keywords
> Links
> Rank
> Results
> Search engine
> Sponsored links

## Resources required

 **Whole Class Presentation: Unit 1.3**

 **Written Task: Keywords**
**Written Task: Keywords (Suggested answers)**

 **Interactive Test: Search engines**

 **Practical Task: Search engines**
**Practical Task: Search engines (Suggested answers)**
**End of Unit Activity: Group research exercise**

**Pages 14–17 of the Pupil's Book**

## Framework reference

Finding things out:

> Using data and information sources: justify the use of an information source
> Searching and selecting: extend and refine search methods to be more efficient

## Teaching notes

1 Use the Module 1 Case Study to introduce pupils to the ways that information can be presented.
2 Use the Whole Class Presentation to explain the objectives of this unit and provide an overview.
3 Ask pupils to look at pages 14 to 17 of the Pupil's Book. This can be projected if facilities exist.
4 Discuss the search engines that pupils currently use and ask them why they use them. Consider other search engines that are available and explain that no one search engine searches all of the web pages available.
5 Pupils complete the Practical Task 'Search engines'.
6 Discuss the answers that pupils have come up with emphasising how some search engines offer different things, e.g. www.ajkids.com is designed specifically for children.
7 Explain how keywords are used to identify relevant sites and how the ranking of hits is based on the number of internal links. Use the diagram on page 16 of the Pupil's Book to demonstrate.
8 Pupils complete the Written Task 'Keywords'.
9 Discuss sponsored links and how the sites that appear at the top might have been sponsored and therefore may not be the most relevant.
10 Pupils complete the Interactive Test.
11 Pupils complete the End of Unit Activity 'Group research', which is partly individual work and partly in groups. You could ask pupils to summarise their research if you don't have time to produce the newspaper article.

## Assessment guidance for End of Unit Activity

**L4** In addition to the criteria detailed in the first paragraph under L4 for Unit 1.2, pupils exchange information and ideas with others in a variety of ways, including using digital communication. They use ICT to organise, store and retrieve information.

Pupils support their conclusion with information from one source. They should not include any information that is clearly implausible although at this level you would not expect them to double check the information with a further source. They copy and paste information from the websites into the document, although they may not summarise or synthesise this information in any way. They may use some of the information at face value without checking it.

They should produce a newspaper article using appropriate software although they may need advice on which software to choose. Their article should be produced in a style that is appropriate for their peers.

**L5** In addition to the L5 criteria given for Unit 1.2, pupils independently select which software to use (either word processing or DTP) and produce a magazine article that is written and designed in a style that is suitable for the audience.

**L6** In addition to the L6 criteria given for Unit 1.2, pupils plan and design ICT-based solutions to meet a specific purpose and audience, demonstrating increased integration and efficiency in their use of ICT tools.

The finished article should very clearly be aimed at people of their age, using design techniques and a style of language that are appropriate.

# 1.4 Teacher's Notes
## Presenting information using a slideshow

## Lesson objectives

This unit combines the processes of searching for information and presenting information. The Pupil's Book is based on an interactive presentation that will be displayed on a console in a museum.

Pupils are asked to consider a standard linear presentation, where one slide is shown after another, and then to consider the idea of hyperlinks that allow the user to navigate around the slideshow for themselves, just viewing the information that they are interested in. This raises the idea of creating a suitable navigation structure.

Pupils research a topic and put an interactive presentation together. Although searching for and evaluating information is not explicitly mentioned in the text, pupils should be reminded to evaluate the validity of any information they use.

## PoS reference

2.1a) consider systematically the information needed to solve a problem, complete a task or answer a question, and explore how it will be used.
2.1b) use and refine search methods to obtain information that is well matched to purpose, by selecting appropriate sources.
2.1c) collect and enter quantitative and qualitative information, checking its accuracy.
2.1d) analyse and evaluate information, judging its value, accuracy, plausibility and bias.
2.2a) select and use ICT tools and techniques appropriately, safely and efficiently.
2.2b) solve problems by developing, exploring and structuring information, and deriving new information for a particular purpose.
2.2f) bring together, draft and refine information, including through the combination of text, sound and image.
2.3a) use a range of ICT tools to present information in forms that are fit for purpose, meet audience needs and suit the content.
2.4a) review, modify and evaluate work as it progresses, reflecting critically and using feedback.
2.4b) reflect on their own and others' uses of ICT to help them develop and improve their ideas and the quality of their work.
3a) use a range of information, with different characteristics, structures and purposes, and evaluation of how it matches requirements and its fitness for purpose.
3b) use a variety of information sources, including large data sets, in a range of contexts.

## STU reference

8.3

## A&A CD-ROM reference

Strand P Activities 1–3
**InteraCT 1 Ref:** Units 1.2, 1.3, 1.4, 1.5, 2.1, 2.2 and 2.3

## PLTS

Independent enquirer
Reflective learner
Creative thinker

## Every Child Matters

Enjoy and achieve
Achieve economic well-being

## Differentiation and inclusion

Levelled worksheets in the Unit
Assessment
Opportunities for group work

## Keywords

> Console
> Hyperlink
> Interactive presentation
> Menu bar
> Presentation
> Slideshow

## Resources required

 **Whole Class Presentation: Unit 1.4**

 **Written Task: Planning a slideshow**

 **Interactive Test: Using slideshows**

 **Practical Task: Adding hyperlinks**
**The history of computers presentation**
**The history of computers (Suggested solution)**
**End of Unit Activity 1.4: Creating an interactive slideshow (L4–5)**
**End of Unit Activity 1.4: Creating an interactive slideshow (L5–6)**

 **Skills Tutorial 1**

**Pages 18–21 of the Pupil's Book**

## Framework reference

Finding things out:

> Using data and information sources: understand how the content and style of an information source affect its suitability for particular purposes

Exchanging and sharing information:

> Fitness for purpose: understand that an effective presentation or publication addresses audience expectations and needs
> Refining and presenting information: plan and design presentations and publications; use a range of ICT tools to combine, refine and present information
> Communicating: understand some of the technical issues involved in efficient electronic communication; use ICT to adapt material for publication to wider or remote audiences

## Teaching notes

1 Use the Module 1 Case Study to introduce pupils to the ways that information can be presented.
2 Use the Whole Class Presentation to explain the objectives of this unit and provide an overview.
3 Ask pupils to look at pages 18 to 21 of the Pupil's Book. This can be projected if facilities exist.
4 Explain the concept of a standard (linear) presentation. Explain the concept of using hyperlinks in presentations (similarly to using them in web pages).
5 Pupils complete the Written Task 'Planning a slideshow'.
6 Demonstrate how to add hyperlinks to slides. Pupils could work through the Skills Tutorial at this stage.
7 Pupils complete the Practical Task 'Adding hyperlinks' using the presentation, 'The history of computers'.
8 Explain the idea of providing the user with easy navigation around a slideshow and discuss circumstances where an interactive slideshow might be appropriate, e.g. on a museum display.
9 Pupils complete the Interactive Test.
10 Pupils create an interactive slideshow using the 'Creating an interactive slideshow' End of Unit Activity worksheet.

## Assessment guidance for End of Unit Activity

**L4** In addition to the criteria detailed in the first paragraph under L4 for Unit 1.2, pupils use ICT to present information in different forms and show they are aware of the intended audience and the need for quality in their presentations. They collect relevant information for their slideshow and although they do not include any implausible information, they do not necessarily double check their sources. They create a slideshow, of at least four slides, that has hyperlinks. They may not have fully considered the navigational structure, for example, they may not have provided links back to the main slide after a link has been followed.

**L5** In addition to the criteria detailed in the first paragraph under L5 for Unit 1.2, pupils should collect relevant information from more than one source and check the accuracy of the information they are using.
   They produce an interactive presentation of four to six slides with a clear navigational structure. They are capable of reviewing other pupils' work and making changes to their own work based on peer review.

**L6** Pupils develop and refine their work to enhance its quality, using a greater range and complexity of information. They present their ideas in a variety of ways and show a clear sense of audience. They use information from several sources and check the validity of the information that they use.
   Pupils create a presentation with a very clear navigation structure in a style that is entirely appropriate for a general museum audience. A key feature at this level is that a range of sources is used. They make meaningful comments about other pupils' work and make changes to their own work after a peer review.

# 1.5 | Teacher's Notes
## Presenting information using audio

## Lesson objectives

This unit develops the work that pupils have done in this module and in Module 1 of InteraCT 1 on searching for information and gathering it to produce some form of presentation, in this case, a news report designed to be broadcast on radio. The key difference with this form of presentation is that they can only use sound and they have a constraint of one minute for their report, which necessitates the careful selection of the information that they want to include.

Pupils are asked to choose from a list of topics that allow for opposing views. Pupils are encouraged to avoid bias and produce a balanced report that covers all sides of the issue.

If you do not have sound-recording and editing software, you can download Audacity free from the Internet. The Windows Sound Recorder can be used although its features are quite limited.

## PoS reference

2.1a) consider systematically the information needed to solve a problem, complete a task or answer a question, and explore how it will be used.

2.1b) use and refine search methods to obtain information that is well matched to purpose, by selecting appropriate sources.

2.1c) collect and enter quantitative and qualitative information, checking its accuracy.

2.1d) analyse and evaluate information, judging its value, accuracy, plausibility and bias.

2.2a) select and use ICT tools and techniques appropriately, safely and efficiently.

2.2f) bring together, draft and refine information, including through the combination of text, sound and image.

2.3a) use a range of ICT tools to present information in forms that are fit for purpose, meet audience needs and suit the content.

2.3b) communicate and exchange information (including digital communication) effectively, safely and responsibly.

2.3c) use technical terms appropriately and correctly.

2.4a) review, modify and evaluate work as it progresses, reflecting critically and using feedback.

2.4b) reflect on their own and others' uses of ICT to help them develop and improve their ideas and the quality of their work.

3a) use a range of information, with different characteristics, structures and purposes, and evaluation of how it matches requirements and its fitness for purpose.

3c) use and review of the effectiveness of different ICT tools, including a range of software applications, in terms of meeting user needs and solving problems.

## STU reference

8.3

## A&A CD-ROM reference

Strand DTP Activities 1–4
**InteraCT 1 Ref:** Units 1.2, 2.1 and 2.2

## PLTS

Independent enquirer
Reflective learner
Creative thinker

## Every Child Matters

Enjoy and achieve
Achieve economic well-being

## Differentiation and inclusion

Levelled worksheets in the Unit Assessment
Opportunities for group work

## Framework reference

See Unit 1.4

## Keywords

> Balanced
> Interview
> News reporting
> Script
> Sound recording software
> Specialist software

## Teaching notes

1 Use the Module 1 Case Study to introduce pupils to the ways that information can be presented.

2 Use the Whole Class Presentation to explain the objectives of this unit and provide an overview.

3 Ask pupils to look at pages 22 to 23 of the Pupil's Book. This can be projected if facilities exist.

4 Introduce pupils to the concept of news reporting and how it is generally unbiased, and balanced.

5 Listen to Radio Script 1 and Radio Script 2 and discuss how reporting does sometimes include bias.

6 Pupils complete the Written Task 'News reports'.

7 Discuss the sources of information that can be used when gathering information, with particular emphasis on the fact that people have different opinions and facts can be disputed.

8 Pupils complete the Interactive Test.

9 Take pupils through the planning process using the checklist on page 23 of the Pupil's Book.

10 Explain how sound can be recorded and demonstrate the software that you will be using.

11 Pupils complete Skills Tutorial 1 or Skills Tutorial 2, depending on the software used.

12 Pupils plan and record their article using the 'Radio news article' End of Unit Activity worksheet.

13 Pupils complete the End of Module Assignment.

## Resources required

 **Whole Class Presentation: Unit 1.5**

 **Written Task: News reports**
**Written Task: News reports (Suggested answers)**

 **Interactive Test: Sources of information**

 **End of Unit Activity 1.5: Radio news article (L4–5)**
**End of Unit Activity 1.5: Radio news article (L5–6)**

 **Skills Tutorials 1–2**

**Pages 22–3 of the Pupil's Book**

## Assessment guidance for End of Unit Activity

**L4** In addition to the criteria given in the first paragraph for this level in Unit 1.2, pupils exchange information and ideas with others in a variety of ways, including using digital communication.

Pupils collect information from one or two sources, to reflect the different views on the topic. They should not include any information that is clearly implausible although at this level you would not expect them to double check the information with a further source. They may use some of the information at face value without checking it. They may need guidance on summarising the information down into a suitable script.

They should produce a radio news item of approximately the right length written in a style that is appropriate for their peers.

**L5** In addition to the criteria given in the first paragraph under L5 for Unit 1.2, pupils exchange information and ideas with others in a variety of ways, including using digital communication.

Pupils use several sources to collect information on their chosen topic. They should attempt to summarise the information, being able to pick out the key points on all sides of the argument. They should need little guidance in planning and recording the article in a style that is suitable for the audience. They may add further appropriate features to the article such as sound effects or backing music.

**L6** Pupils plan and design ICT-based solutions to meet a specific purpose and audience, demonstrating increased integration and efficiency in their use of ICT tools. They develop and refine their work to enhance its quality, using a greater range and complexity of information. Where necessary, they use complex lines of enquiry to test hypotheses. They present their ideas in a variety of ways and show a clear sense of audience.

At this level, pupils should use multiple sources to ensure that they have covered all aspects of their chosen topic. The information should be balanced and reliable. The key characteristic at this level is that several sources of information are used. Sources should be quoted with some indication of why they trust this particular source.

The finished article should very clearly be aimed at people of their age, using design techniques and a style of language that are appropriate. They are likely to include other relevant features such as interviews, sound effects, or backing or introductory music.

DL *DYNAMIC LEARNING* © Hodder Education 2008

# 2 | Teacher's Notes
## Web design and creation

## Module structure

Web design and creation were not covered in the InteraCT 1 course so pupils are introduced to it for the first time. However, web design has much in common with the work that pupils did on presentations in InteraCT 1. The emphasis on this module therefore is to focus on issues that are specific to structuring, designing and creating a website.

2.1 Reviewing web page design
2.2 Methods for creating web pages
2.3 Creating a web page using HTML
2.4 Creating a web page using specialised software
2.5 Structuring a website

In Unit 2.1, pupils evaluate web page design, relating back to purpose and audience (covered in InteraCT 1). They also look at specific issues relating to websites, such as navigation. Units 2.2 to 2.4 look at the ways that pupils can create websites and the pros and cons of each method. Unit 2.2 introduces the three main ways (HTML, standard software, specialised software). Unit 2.3 covers the basic of HTML and Unit 2.4 uses FrontPage as an example of specialised software that can be used. Unit 2.5 covers some of the issues that arise as websites start to grow in terms of creating a suitable structure and navigation method around the site.

As with all the modules, there are some module resources that you can use before you start on the units. These are:

> Module 2 Case Study
> Module 2 Starter Activities

## Assessment

Most assessments in this module are designed to allow pupils to demonstrate levels 4 to 6. Some of the units only cover levels 4 to 5 as they introduce topics not covered in Year 7. There are levelled Unit Assessments and interpretation of the levels is provided in the Teacher's Notes for each unit.

There is also a levelled Module Assignment that pupils can work on when all the units are complete. This is designed to cover all aspects of this module. This is a differentiated activity and you should give each pupil the worksheet that is most appropriate to the level that you think they are working towards. The interpretation of levels for the Module Assignment is given below.

## Assessment guidance for Module Assignment

**L4** Pupils add to, amend and combine different forms of information from a variety of sources. They use ICT to present information in different forms and show they are aware of the intended audience and the need for quality in their presentations. They exchange information and ideas with others in a variety of ways, including using digital communication. They use ICT to organise, store and retrieve information.

Pupils create a suitable plan for their website in diagrammatical form. They also produce a plan for their home page. Their plan should include references to all of the web pages and sections listed in the brief, although it may not be the best solution.

Pupils should be able to create a website which shows some consistency in terms of design. It should be written in a style that is suitable for its purpose. The website may be limited to fairly basic features within the software.

**L5** Pupils use ICT to structure, refine and present information in different forms and styles for specific purposes and audiences. They exchange information and ideas with others in a variety of ways, including using digital communications. They use ICT to organise, store and retrieve information using logical and appropriate structures.

A pupil who is clearly working at L5 would benefit from working on the L5/6 variant of the worksheet as it gives more open-ended instructions.

Pupils present a good plan for the website including all of the sections and pages required. Their home page shows clearly how to navigate to the various sections and pages.

Pupils design and produce the website showing a clear awareness of the purpose of the pages. They include features that they have observed on other sites. They may include additional features such as sound and video content.

**L6** Pupils develop and refine their work to enhance its quality, using a greater range and complexity of information.

Pupils demonstrate an ability to plan the content and structure of the website with very little information. They should be able to work out what pages and sections might be needed for a site such as this.

The instructions are deliberately open-ended to allow pupils to interpret the requirements and create an appropriate website in response. They work autonomously to produce a website that is clearly written and designed in a style suitable for this purpose and audience. The site should be easy to navigate and should show use of themes and styles for consistency.

# Suggested answers to questions posed in the Case Study

**Q** What is the purpose of their website? Who is the audience for their website?

**Suggested answers:**
The purpose is to inform people about the services they offer and persuade them to buy them.
The audience is people aged from 18 to 21.

**Q** What do you like about the design of these pages? What problems might there be with the design of these two pages?

**Suggested answers:**
Pupils may comment on:

> the inconsistency of the design
> use of different colours on each page
> use of different font sizes and styles on each page
> a lack of visual interest, e.g. lack of images
> difficulty in navigating around the site, i.e. lack of clear hyperlinks.

**Q** How clear is the information on the page? Does it give you all the information you need?

**Suggested answers:**
Pupils may comment on:

> lack of information about the range of clothing on offer
> lack of pictures
> very vague information about size, prices and availability.

**Q** What software or tools could Zoe use to create the website? Why might she choose one method rather than another?

**Suggested answers:**
> HTML
> Word
> Publisher
> FrontPage
> Dreamweaver
> Any other suitable software, including web-based tools.

**Q** What would be the best way to create the links on each page?

**Suggested answers:**
Pupils may suggest:

> adding links to text or images
> using buttons
> using tabs
> pupils may comment on the consistent use of links on each page to aid navigation.

**Q** In what ways is Zoe's new design an improvement on the original web pages?

**Suggested answers:**
Pupils may comment on:

> consistent use of colours and fonts
> consistent layout
> ease of navigation through consistent use of hyperlinks
> use of a design that is more appealing to the audience.

# 2.1 Teacher's Notes
## Reviewing web page design

## Lesson objectives

This unit focuses on the design of websites in terms of the layout, navigation and clarity of web pages. Pupils should be reminded that a web page is a way of presenting information and that all of the things they learnt about presenting information in InteraCT 1 and in Module 1 also apply here.

Pupils think about the way in which web pages are designed to appeal to specific audiences and look at some examples and identify the differences for themselves.

Pupils consider the navigation features of websites in terms of tools, such as hyperlinks and tabs, but also in terms of consistent design features that help the user to find what they are looking for. Finally, pupils consider the importance of clarity in the way that information is presented.

## PoS reference

2.2d) design information systems and suggest improvements to existing systems.

2.2f) bring together, draft and refine information, including through the combination of text, sound and image.

2.3b) communicate and exchange information (including digital communication) effectively, safely and responsibly.

2.3c) use technical terms appropriately and correctly.

2.4b) reflect on their own and others' uses of ICT to help them develop and improve their ideas and the quality of their work.

## Framework reference

Exchanging and sharing information:

> Fitness for purpose: understand that an effective presentation or publication addresses audience expectations and needs; evaluate the effectiveness of publications and presentations
> Refining and presenting information: plan and design presentations and publications

## STU reference

8.2

## A&A CD-ROM reference

Strand WB Activities 1–2

## PLTS

Independent enquirer
Reflective learner
Creative thinker

## Every Child Matters

Enjoy and achieve
Achieve economic well-being

## Differentiation and inclusion

None in this unit as it is an introductory unit

## Keywords

> Clarity
> Design
> Navigate
> Navigation
> Tab
> Thumbnail
> Upload
> Web page
> Website

## Resources required

**Whole Class Presentation: Unit 2.1**

**Written Task: Web page design**
**Written Task: Web page design  (Suggested answers)**

**Interactive Test: Web page design**

**Practical Task: Purpose and audience**
**Practical Task: Purpose and audience (Suggested answers)**
**End of Unit Activity 2.1: Canoe club website evaluation**
**Canoe club website**

**Pages 28–31 of the Pupil's Book**

## Teaching notes

1 Use the Module 2 Case Study to introduce pupils to the ways that information can be presented.
2 Use the Whole Class Presentation to explain the objectives of this unit and provide an overview.
3 Recap on the importance of purpose and audience when considering the presentation of any information regardless of the format.
4 Pupils complete the Practical Task 'Purpose and audience'.
5 Pupils complete the Interactive Test on purpose and audience.
6 Show pupils the CBeebies web pages on page 29 of the Pupil's Book and ask them to spot the similarities between the two pages. Discuss the design features and how they appeal to a very young audience.
7 Pupils complete the Written Task 'Web page design'.
8 Discuss the concept of navigation. Show pupils the YouTube website (or any other suitable website) where there is a clear navigational structure provided.
9 Discuss the concept of clarity of information in relation to audience needs. Project the BBC news web page and highlight differences in the amount of information and number of links from this page.
10 Pupils complete the End of Unit Activity 'Canoe club website evaluation'.

## Assessment guidance for End of Unit Activity

This unit primarily deals with the evaluation of web page design and with suggesting changes to web pages or re-designing web pages by hand. In terms of levels, this does not go beyond L4/5, but is a necessary starting point for later units. It is not possible for pupils to meet any of the level statements in their entirety. However, the subsequent units in this module require pupils to create web pages from scratch giving them the opportunity to demonstrate capability more fully across levels 4 to 6.

**L4** Pupils use ICT to generate, develop, organise and present their work.

Pupils can demonstrate some capability at this level by making suggestions of changes that could be made to the website. Their suggestions should show improvements to the overall design and layout, but may not take account of the audience.

**L5** Pupils use ICT to present information in different forms and show they are aware of the intended audience and the need for quality in their presentations.

Pupils can partially demonstrate this by suggesting changes to the Canoe club website that would make it more suitable for the target audience (young people who they are trying to persuade to join the club). For example, they might make suggestions about changing the layout, using different font styles and colours, or reducing the amount of text on each page.

# 2.2 | Teacher's Notes
## Methods for creating web pages

## Lesson objectives

This unit focuses on the tools that are available for the creation of web pages. The main purpose of the unit is to explain the three main options and to get pupils to make choices about which tools they would use.

The unit includes an introduction to HTML, though pupils are not expected to write any HTML code. Pupils also consider the use of Word and Publisher for web design and go on to look at specialised software that is available, in particular FrontPage.

## PoS reference

2.2a) select and use ICT tools and techniques appropriately, safely and efficiently.

2.4b) reflect on their own and others' uses of ICT to help them develop and improve their ideas and the quality of their work.

2.4c) reflect on what they have learnt and use these insights to improve future work.

3c) use and review of the effectiveness of different ICT tools, including a range of software applications, in terms of meeting user needs and solving problems.

## Framework reference

Exchanging and sharing information:

> Refining and presenting information: plan and design presentations and publications; use a range of ICT tools to combine, refine and present information

## Resources required

**Whole Class Introduction: Unit 2.2**

**Written Task: HTML**
**Written Task: HTML (Answers)**
**Code for horse web page**
**HTML version of horse web page**

**Interactive Test: Creating web pages**

**Practical Task: Comparing methods**
**Practical Task: Comparing methods (Suggested answers)**
**Horse web page created in Word**
**Files for  horse web page created in Word**
**Horse web page created in Publisher**
**Files for horse web page created in Publisher**
**HTML version of horse web page created in Publisher**
**End of Unit Activity 2.2: Creating a web page**

**Skills Tutorials 1–3    Pages 32–5 of the Pupil's Book**

## STU reference

8.2

## A&A CD-ROM reference

Strand WB Activities 1–2

## PLTS

Independent enquirer
Reflective learner
Creative thinker

## Every Child Matters

Enjoy and achieve
Achieve economic well-being

## Differentiation and inclusion

Levelled worksheets in the Unit Assessment

## Keywords

> Browser
> Code
> HTML
> HTML format
> Mark-up language
> Specialist software
> Standard software

# Teaching notes

1 Use the Module 2 Case Study to introduce pupils to the ways that information can be presented.
2 Use the Whole Class Presentation to explain the objectives of this unit and provide an overview.
3 Discuss the three main ways of creating web pages: HTML coding, standard software and specialised software. Question pupils to see if they know of any other web development tools.
4 Demonstrate basic HTML coding using the screenshots on pages 32–3 of the Pupil's Book. Pick out a couple of examples. Not too much detail is needed here depending on your own knowledge of HTML.
5 Pupils complete the Written Task 'HTML'.
6 Discuss the use of Word and Publisher for web page creation.
7 Pupils complete the Practical Task 'Comparing methods'.
8 Pupils may need to work through the first two Skills Tutorials on how to use Word and Publisher for web page creation.
9 Discuss the use of specialist software such as FrontPage or Dreamweaver.
10 Pupils can complete Skills Tutorial 3 on creating a page in FrontPage.
11 Discuss all of the options and decide which method you might use.
12 Pupils complete the Interactive Test.
13 Pupils complete the End of Unit Activity 'Creating a web page'.

# Assessment guidance for End of Unit Activity

In this unit, pupils are asked to produce a simple web page and justify the selection of the chosen method for producing the page. As this unit introduces the methods, pupils cannot demonstrate full capability at any level, but can show partial attainment at L4 and L5. In subsequent units of this module, they can demonstrate capability up to L6.

**L4** Pupils use ICT to present information in different forms and show they are aware of the intended audience and the need for quality in their presentations. They exchange information and ideas with others in a variety of ways, including using digital communication.

Pupils can demonstrate some capability of presenting and exchanging information through the creation of the web page using their chosen method. They should need little assistance and provide sensible reasons why they chose the method they did.

**L5** Pupils use ICT to structure, refine and present information in different forms and styles for specific purposes and audiences. They exchange information and ideas with others in a variety of ways, including using digital communication.

Pupils can show some evidence of presenting and exchanging information requiring no assistance in creating the web page using their chosen method. They provide detailed explanations of why they chose that particular method.

# 2.3 Teacher's Notes
## Creating a web page using HTML

## Lesson objectives

This unit focuses on the use of HTML code to create web pages. It is not necessary for pupils to know a lot of HTML, but just to have a working knowledge of the basic constructs of the language. This unit could be developed further if you feel confident with HTML. If not, this unit gives pupils all the instructions they need to make a simple web page with some text, an image and a hyperlink.

Pupils may conclude from working with HTML that it is easier and more efficient to work with a standard or specialised program to create web pages. The use of HTML serves as a good introduction to the concept of mark-up languages and the fact that all computer programs have code behind the user interface to make them work.

## PoS reference

2.2a) select and use ICT tools and techniques appropriately, safely and efficiently.

2.4b) reflect on their own and others' uses of ICT to help them develop and improve their ideas and the quality of their work.

2.4c) reflect on what they have learnt and use these insights to improve future work.

3c) use and review of the effectiveness of different ICT tools, including a range of software applications, in terms of meeting user needs and solving problems.

## Framework reference

Developing ideas and making things happen:

> Analysing and automating processes: automate simple processes

Exchanging and sharing information:

> Refining and presenting information: plan and design presentations and publications; use a range of ICT tools to combine, refine and present information

## STU reference

8.2

## A&A CD-ROM reference

Strand WB Activities 1–2

## PLTS

Independent enquirer
Reflective learner
Creative thinker

## Every Child Matters

Enjoy and achieve
Achieve economic well-being

## Differentiation and inclusion

Levelled worksheets in the Unit Assessment
Opportunities for self-review

## Keywords

> Browser
> Internet Explorer
> Mozilla
> Notepad
> Tags
> Text editor

## Resources required

 **Whole Class Presentation: Unit 2.3**

 **Written Task: Cracking the code**
**Written Task: Cracking the code (Suggested answer in Notepad)**
**Written Task: Cracking the code (Suggested answer in HTML)**
**Written Task: Cracking the code (HTML file)**

 **Interactive Test: HTML tags**

 **End of Unit Activity 2.3: My favourite websites (L4–5)**
**End of Unit Activity 2.3: My favourite websites (L5–6)**
**Self-Review Sheet**

 **Skills Tutorial 1**

**Pages 36–7 of the Pupil's Book**

## Teaching notes

1 Use the Module 2 Case Study to introduce pupils to the ways that information can be presented.
2 Use the Whole Class Presentation to explain the objectives of this unit and provide an overview.
3 Explain the basic principle of HTML and the use of mark-up languages in general. Explain how this code 'sits behind' every web page they look at.
4 Use the examples from the presentation or from pages 36 to 37 of the Pupil's Book to show the basic syntax of HTML code, i.e. the use of tags.
5 Pupils interpret some code through the Written Task 'Cracking the code'.
6 Pupils complete the Interactive Test.
7 Remind pupils about hyperlinks and explain how to add them in HTML.
8 Pupils complete the final assessment using the End of Unit Activity 'My favourite websites' worksheet.
9 Pupils may need to work through the Skills Tutorial at this point, which shows them how to type basic commands into Notepad and save them in HTML format.

## Assessment guidance for End of Unit Activity

In this unit, pupils are asked to produce a web page and consider the suitability of using HTML for web page creation. Pupils can show that they are working towards Levels 4 and 5, with some evidence of L6 possible in this task.

**L4** Pupils use ICT to present information in different forms and show they are aware of the intended audience and the need for quality in their presentations. They exchange information and ideas with others in a variety of ways, including using digital communication.

Pupils should be able to create a web page that demonstrates some of the standard features of HTML. At this level, they may create a single page. They should write the text in a style that is appropriate for their peers. They should be able to comment on the use of HTML as a method of web page production although this may be at a fairly superficial level.

**L5** Pupils use ICT to structure, refine and present information in different forms and styles for specific purposes and audiences. They exchange information and ideas with others in a variety of ways, including using digital communication.

Pupils should be able to create a web page that demonstrates a good grasp of basic HTML. They should create more than one page, with links between the pages, and the external links all working correctly. Their design should show an awareness of the audience. They should make sensible comments in their self-review, identifying some of the limitations of using HTML.

**L6** Pupils present their ideas in a variety of ways and show a clear sense of audience. Pupils can show some evidence at this level if they are able to work largely unaided in putting together a three-page website. A feature at this level is that they will explore HTML code autonomously in order to find out how to do things that they have not been told how to do yet.

# 2.4 Teacher's Notes
## Creating a web page using specialised software

## Lesson objectives

This is a very hands-on unit focusing on the use of specialised software to create web pages. In particular, it uses FrontPage although the activities can be completed in any web design software.

Pupils will probably find it easier to build web pages in specialised software and the quality of their finished pages should be higher than the HTML ones they created in Unit 2.3.

Pupils are encouraged to plan their web pages before they start and the importance of consistency of design is stressed. Some specific features of web design software are covered though pupils should be encouraged to explore the other tools available.

## PoS reference

2.1a) consider systematically the information needed to solve a problem, complete a task or answer a question, and explore how it will be used.

2.2a) select and use ICT tools and techniques appropriately, safely and efficiently.

2.2d) design information systems and suggest improvements to existing systems.

2.2f) bring together, draft and refine information, including through the combination of text, sound and image.

2.3a) use a range of ICT tools to present information in forms that are fit for purpose, meet audience needs and suit the content.

2.3b) communicate and exchange information (including digital communication) effectively, safely and responsibly.

2.3c) use technical terms appropriately and correctly.

2.4a) review, modify and evaluate work as it progresses, reflecting critically and using feedback.

2.4b) reflect on their own and others' uses of ICT to help them develop and improve their ideas and the quality of their work.

3c) use and review of the effectiveness of different ICT tools, including a range of software applications, in terms of meeting user needs and solving problems.

## Framework reference

Developing ideas and making things happen:

> Analysing and automating processes: automate simple processes; consider the benefits and drawbacks of using ICT to automate processes; represent simple design specifications as diagrams

Exchanging and sharing information:

> Fitness for purpose: understand that an effective presentation or publication addresses audience expectations and needs; evaluate the effectiveness of publications and presentations
> Refining and presenting information: plan and design presentations and publications; use a range of ICT tools to combine, refine and present information

## STU reference

8.2

## A&A CD-ROM reference

Strand WB Activities 1–2

## PLTS

Independent enquirer
Reflective learner
Creative thinker

## Every Child Matters

Enjoy and achieve
Achieve economic well-being

## Differentiation and inclusion

Levelled worksheets in the Unit
Assessment
Opportunities for peer- and self-review

## Keywords

> Button
> Styles
> Themes
> Wizard

## Resources required

 **Whole Class Presentation: Unit 2.4**

 **Written Task: Designing a personal web page**

 **Interactive Test: Web design software**

 **Practical Task: Creating a personal web page**
**End of Unit Activity 2.4: Developing a website (L4–5)**
**End of Unit Activity 2.4: Developing a website (L5–6)**

 **Skills Tutorials 1–3**

**Pages 38–41 of the Pupil's Book**

## Teaching notes

1 Use the Module 2 Case Study to introduce pupils to the ways that information can be presented.
2 Use the Whole Class Presentation to explain the objectives of this unit and provide an overview.
3 Recap on the concept of using specialised web design software as opposed to generic software (such as Word) and HTML coding. Ask pupils if they know any web design tools.
4 There are three Skills Tutorials which pupils can work through either in stages or all in one go.
5 Pupils complete the hand-drawn designs for a web page (Written Task) and go straight on to create them using whatever web design software you have available (Practical Task).
6 When complete, discuss adding pages together to make a website. Discuss the implications in terms of consistency of design and thinking about how the links work between the pages.
7 Pupils complete the Interactive Test.
8 Pupils complete the End of Unit Activity 'Developing a website', which builds on the Written Task and Practical Task.

## Assessment guidance for End of Unit Activity

**L4** Pupils add to, amend and combine different forms of information from a variety of sources. They use ICT to present information in different forms and show they are aware of the intended audience and the need for quality in their presentations.

Pupils should be able to put together a three-page website which shows some consistency in terms of design. It should be written in a style that is suitable for its purpose. It would be acceptable, for example, for pupils to use TXT language as this is common on social networking sites. The website may be limited to fairly basic features within the software.

**L5** Pupils use ICT to structure, refine and present information in different forms and styles for specific purposes and audiences.

A clear L5 pupil would benefit from working on the L5/6 variant of this worksheet as this gives more open-ended instructions. Pupils design and produce the website showing a clear awareness of the purpose of the pages. They include features that they have observed on other (social networking) sites. They may include additional features such as sound and video content.

**L6** Pupils present their ideas in a variety of ways and show a clear sense of audience.

The instructions at L6 are deliberately open-ended to allow pupils to interpret the requirements and create an appropriate website in response. They work autonomously to produce a website that is clearly written and designed in a style suitable for this purpose and audience. The site should be easy to navigate and use themes and styles for consistency.

 DL DYNAMIC LEARNING © Hodder Education 2008

# 2.5 Teacher's Notes
## Structuring a website

## Lesson objectives

This unit focuses specifically on the structure of websites and explains the three main ways in which sites are structured: linear, tree and random. Pupils are asked to consider which structure would be the most suitable in different circumstances, and even that a site may contain sections that are structured differently.

Pupils are not required to create a website in this unit, but are required to represent the structure of a website in the form of a diagram. Example diagrams are shown in the Pupil's Book though other formats would be acceptable.

Pupils also consider the way that hyperlinks are shown on a typical page, and the way in which most sites use several methods to make it quick and easy for users to find the pages they are interested in.

## PoS reference

2.2a) select and use ICT tools and techniques appropriately, safely and efficiently.

2.2f) bring together, draft and refine information, including through the combination of text, sound and image.

2.3b) communicate and exchange information (including digital communication) effectively, safely and responsibly.

2.3c) use technical terms appropriately and correctly.

3c) use and review of the effectiveness of different ICT tools, including a range of software applications, in terms of meeting user needs and solving problems.

## Framework reference

Finding things out:

> Using data and information sources: understand how the content and style of an information source affect its suitability for particular purposes

Developing ideas and making things happen:

> Analysing and automating processes: represent simple design specifications as diagrams

Exchanging and sharing information:

> Fitness for purpose: understand that an effective presentation or publication addresses audience expectations and needs
> Refining and presenting information: plan and design presentations and publications; use a range of ICT tools to combine, refine and present information
> Communicating: understand some of the technical issues involved in efficient electronic communication; use ICT to adapt material for publication to wider or remote audiences

## STU reference

8.2

## A&A CD-ROM reference

Strand WB Activities 1–2

## PLTS

Independent enquirer
Reflective learner
Creative thinker

## Every Child Matters

Enjoy and achieve
Achieve economic well-being

## Differentiation and inclusion

Levelled worksheets in the Unit Assessment
Opportunities for peer- and self-review

## Keywords

> Application form
> Linear
> Online form
> Online shopping
> Random
> Tabs
> Tree
> Website section
> Website structure

## Resources required

 **Whole Class Presentation: Unit 2.5**

 **Written Task: Website structures**
**Written Task: Website structures (Suggested answers)**
**End of Unit Activity 2.5: Structuring a website (L4–5)**
**End of Unit Activity 2.5: Structuring a website (L5–6)**

 **Interactive Test: Website structures**

**Pages 42–5 of the Pupil's Book**

## Teaching notes

1 Use the Module 2 Case Study to introduce pupils to the ways that information can be presented.
2 Use the Whole Class Presentation to explain the objectives of this unit and provide an overview.
3 You should spend some time discussing the three main structures explaining the possible routes through each, for example, which pages are directly linked and which are not. Stress the importance of planning.
4 Discuss how the structure depends on the website. Discuss some examples and ask pupils for others.
5 Pupils complete the 'Website structures' worksheet (Written Task) and go straight on to the Interactive Test, both of which are on the same theme.
6 Project a web page (if facilities exist) or ask pupils to look at the one on page 45 of the Pupil's Book. Discuss all the ways in which links are added to a page.
7 Pupils complete the End of Unit Activity 'Structuring a website', which builds on the Written Task and Interactive Test.
8 Pupils complete the End of Module Assignment.

## Assessment guidance for End of Unit Activity

Pupils do not need to create a full website for this activity, so they cannot fully achieve any of the level descriptions. However, their planning of the website and home page meets part of the level descriptions at Levels 4 to 6.

**L4** Pupils use ICT to present information in different forms and show they are aware of the intended audience and the need for quality in their presentations. They exchange information and ideas with others in a variety of ways, including using digital communication. They use ICT to organise, store and retrieve information.

Pupils create a suitable plan for their website in diagrammatic form. They also produce a plan for their home page. Their plan should include references to all of the web pages and sections listed in the brief, although it may not be the best solution.

**L5** Pupils use ICT to structure, refine and present information in different forms and styles for specific purposes and audiences. They exchange information and ideas with others in a variety of ways, including using digital communications. They use ICT to organise, store and retrieve information using logical and appropriate structures.

Pupils present a good plan for the website including all of the sections and pages required. Their home page clearly shows how to navigate to the various sections and pages.

**L6** Pupils develop and refine their work to enhance its quality, using a greater range and complexity of information.

A feature of L6 is the ability to plan the contents and the structure of the website with very little information. They should be able to work out what pages and sections might be needed for a typical secondary school.

# 3 | Teacher's Notes
## Modelling

## Module structure

Modelling was covered in InteraCT 1 and this module aims to extend and develop pupils' capabilities beyond the basics. The focus of the unit is on creating models from scratch, making them as accurate and realistic as possible. Pupils also look at the concept of using models to simulate real life and create their own simulations.

3.1 Creating a spreadsheet model
3.2 Developing a model to improve accuracy
3.3 Using graphs to model data
3.4 Using simulations
3.5 Creating a simulation

Unit 3.1 starts with a recap on spreadsheet basics and pupils then go on to create a model from scratch. Unit 3.2 focuses on reviewing and refining the model to make it as accurate and realistic as possible. Unit 3.3 looks at the way in which graphs can be used to model situations. Finally, Units 3.4 and 3.5 concentrate on using and then creating models which can be used to simulate real life.

As with all the modules, there are some module resources that you can use before you start on the units. These are:

> Module 3 Case Study
> Module 3 Starter Activities

## Assessment

Most assessments in this module are designed to allow pupils to demonstrate levels 4 to 6. There are levelled Unit Assessments and interpretation of the levels is provided in the Teacher's Notes for each unit.

There is also a levelled Module Assignment that pupils can work on when all the units are complete. This is designed to cover all aspects of this module. This is a differentiated activity and you should give each pupil the worksheet that is most appropriate to the level that you think they are working towards. The interpretation of levels for the Module Assignment is given below.

## Assessment guidance for Module Assignment

**L4** Pupils use ICT-based models and simulations to explore patterns and relationships, and make predictions about the consequences of their decisions. They use ICT to organise, store and retrieve information.

L4 pupils may need considerable guidance in scoping the problem and setting up the spreadsheet model in the first instance. You may need to show them the suggested solution to give them an idea of how to get started. Once they have the basic structure they should be able to add suitable formulae and create a graph largely unaided.

**L5** Pupils explore the effects of changing the variables in an ICT-based model. They use ICT to

organise, store and retrieve information using logical and appropriate structures.

L5 pupils may need some guidance in setting up the spreadsheet model but will then work largely unaided. They should be able to create a realistic model and create the graphs needed.

**L6** Pupils use ICT-based models to make predictions and vary the rules within the models. They assess the validity of these models by comparing their behaviour with information from other sources.

A characteristic of L6 is the ability of the pupil to set up the spreadsheet from scratch with little or no help. In addition, they should add other factors to the model that they think will make it more realistic.

# Suggested answers to questions posed in the Case Study

**Q** Why might Harriet need more staff when the diner is busy? When do you think the busiest times and days are likely to be?

**Suggested answers:**
Harriet may need more staff when the diner is busy as one member of staff is only physically capable of serving a certain number of customers. Busy times in restaurants tend to be lunchtimes and evenings. Weekends are likely to be busier than weekdays as fewer people are at work or school.

**Q** If you were Harriet, how would you work out how many staff to have working on different days of the week?

**Suggested answers:**
Harriet should look at the number of customers that she typically gets in the diner on different days of the week. She could look at an average figure and use this to work out how many waiters or waitresses she would need on the average day. She could also look at the total number of people and see what the range is e.g. between 200 and 250 people.

**Q** Can you see any pattern in the data? Which days seem to be the busiest? How can this help Harriet work out how many staff to have on each day?

**Suggested answers:**
Monday, Tuesday and Wednesday seem to be the quietest days with between 200 and 300 customers. It gets busier on a Thursday and Friday with between 300 and 400 customers. Saturday is busier still and Sunday is the busiest day with up to 1000 customers.

Harriet knows that she needs one member of staff for each 80 customers. If she divides the total number by 80, she can work out how many staff she needs.

**Q** How else could Harriet present these data to make them easier to read?

**Suggested answers:**
In graph form, as a line chart or bar chart.

**Q** Which are the quietest days of the week? How many customers do they get on a typical Tuesday? How many customers do they get on a typical Saturday?

**Suggested answers:**
Monday, Tuesday and Wednesday are the quietest days. There are typically between 200 and 300 on a Tuesday and between 600 and 700 on a Saturday.

**Q** How many staff do you think Harriet needs for a typical Monday?

**Suggested answers:**
Either 3 or 4 staff.

**Q** How realistic do you think a model like this is? How could the model be extended to be even more useful to Harriet? What other situations could be modelled in this way?

**Suggested answers:**
The model is realistic if Harriet's original figures are correct and if she is right about needing one member of staff per 80 customers. She has only looked at customer numbers for 4 weeks and it might be more accurate to look at the numbers over a longer period.

Harriet could extend the model to include different times of the day. If the waiters or waitresses work in shifts, she could work out how many she needs at different times of the day, e.g. lunchtime and dinner time will be busier than mid-morning or mid-afternoon.

There are many situations that could be modelled in this way:

> Any shop or business that has customers could use a model like this to predict numbers.
> Harriet could make a model to predict how much money she might make or how many products she might sell.
> Harriet could predict what supplies she needs to buy each week so that she does not run out.

# 3.1 Teacher's Notes
## Creating a spreadsheet model

## Lesson objectives

In this unit, pupils are expected to create spreadsheet models. This unit builds directly on the work that pupils did in Module 3 in InteraCT 1 and includes an online task as a reminder of the basics of modelling. It is assumed that pupils have an understanding of the basics and are able to set up basic spreadsheets using simple formulae.

The focus is on pupils being able to identify the variables and rules that are used in models. Pupils work through an entire model, being shown the variables and rules, and then create one for themselves in the Unit Assessment.

## PoS reference

2.2c) test predictions and discover patterns and relationships, exploring, evaluating and developing models by changing their rules and values.
2.2d) design information systems and suggest improvements to existing systems.

## Framework reference

Finding things out:

> Organising and investigating: explore and interpret collected data in order to draw conclusions

Developing ideas and making things happen:

> Models and modelling: develop ICT-based models and test predictions; draw and explain conclusions; improve the accuracy and extend the scope of ICT models

## Resources required

**Whole Class Presentation: Unit 3.1**

**Written Task: Identifying variables worksheet**
**Written Task: Identifying variables (Suggested answers)**

**Interactive Test: Spreadsheet modelling**

**End of Unit Activity 3.1: Setting up a model (L4-5)**
**End of Unit Activity 3.1: Setting up a model (L5-6)**
**End of Unit Activity 3.1: Setting up a model (Answers)**
**Concert hall evacuation spreadsheet**
**Concert hall evacuation spreadsheet (Suggested solution)**

**Inks R Us spreadsheet**
**Mobile phone model**

**Pages 50–3 of the Pupil's Book**

## STU reference

8.4

## A&A CD-ROM reference

Strand M Activities 1–4
**InteraCT 1 Ref:** Module 3

## PLTS

Independent enquirer
Reflective learner

## Every Child Matters

Enjoy and achieve
Achieve economic well-being

## Differentiation and inclusion

Levelled worksheets in the Unit Assessment
Opportunities for peer- and self-review

## Keywords

> Predictions
> Rules
> Variables
> What if

# Teaching notes

1 Use the Module 3 Case Study to introduce pupils to the ways in which modelling is used in real situations, if necessary.
2 Use the Whole Class Presentation to explain the objectives of this unit and provide an overview of the main concept of creating a spreadsheet model.
3 Recap on spreadsheet basics and on the use of models. Use any spreadsheet model as an example, such as the 'Inks R Us' model, or the 'Mobile Phone' model referred to in the Pupil's Book.
4 Pupils complete the Interactive Test of existing knowledge. Pupils struggling with this may benefit from revisiting the InteraCT 1 course.
5 Explain the concept of variables. Use any model as an example.
6 Pupils complete the Written Task 'Identifying variables'.
7 Explain the concept of rules. Use any model as an example.
8 Pupils complete the End of Unit Activity 'Setting up a model'.

# Assessment guidance for End of Unit Activity

The creation of spreadsheets allows pupils to demonstrate capability across Levels 4 to 6. The emphasis of this unit is on Levels 5 and 6.

**L4** Pupils use ICT-based models and simulations to explore patterns and relationships, and make predictions about the consequences of their decisions.

At L4, you could provide pupils with the basic template, which contains the variables without any values or rules (formulae). Pupils should be able to make changes to create the spreadsheet largely unaided.

They should be able to answer the first two questions with little help but the last two questions are more difficult. A typical response for Q4 would be to try several values in the 'number of exits' cell until the desired answer was achieved.

**L5** Pupils explore the effects of changing the variables in an ICT-based model.

A capable L5 pupil should be given the L5/6 version of the worksheet, which requires them to set the model up from scratch. Pupils should be able to create the spreadsheet unaided and all formulae should be tested so that the spreadsheet works fully. L5 pupils should be able to tackle all questions on the worksheet although their answers to the final question may be cursory. A feature of L5 and above would be the use of 'goal seek' to answer Q5.

**L6** Pupils use ICT-based models to make predictions and vary the rules within the models. They assess the validity of these models by comparing their behaviour with information from other sources.
Pupils should be able to create the model from scratch, identifying the variables and the rules needed to answer the questions. They can answer all of the questions largely unaided.

# 3.2 Teacher's Notes
## Developing a model to improve accuracy

## Lesson objectives

This unit focuses specifically on developing models to make sure that they are accurate, reliable and produce a valid result. Pupils look further at the 'Concert Hall Evacuation model' introduced in Unit 3.1 and are shown how to make changes to improve its accuracy and realism. Pupils evaluate and develop the mobile phone model to include more factors and make it more realistic.

In terms of skills, pupils are shown how to add drop-down lists and how to use a basic 'If' statement to take account of different circumstances.

## PoS reference

2.1a) consider systematically the information needed to solve a problem, complete a task or answer a question, and explore how it will be used.
2.1c) collect and enter quantitative and qualitative information, checking its accuracy.
2.1d) analyse and evaluate information, judging its value, accuracy, plausibility and bias.
2.2a) select and use ICT tools and techniques appropriately, safely and efficiently.
2.2b) solve problems by developing, exploring and structuring information, and deriving new information for a particular purpose.
2.2c) test predictions and discover patterns and relationships, exploring, evaluating and developing models by changing their rules and values.
2.2d) design information systems and suggest improvements to existing systems.
2.4a) review, modify and evaluate work as it progresses, reflecting critically and using feedback.
2.4b) reflect on their own and others' uses of ICT to help them develop and improve their ideas and the quality of their work.
2.4c) reflect on what they have learnt and use these insights to improve future work.
3c) use and review of the effectiveness of different ICT tools, including a range of software applications, in terms of meeting user needs and solving problems.

## Framework reference

Finding things out:

> Organising and investigating: explore and interpret collected data in order to draw conclusions

Developing ideas and making things happen:

> Models and modelling: develop ICT-based models and test predictions; draw and explain conclusions; improve the accuracy and extend the scope of ICT models

## STU reference

8.4

## A&A CD-ROM reference

Strand M Activities 1–4
**InteraCT 1 Ref:** Module 3

## PLTS

Independent enquirer
Reflective learner

## Every Child Matters

Enjoy and achieve
Achieve economic well-being

## Differentiation and inclusion

Levelled worksheets in the Unit Assessment
Opportunities for peer- and self-review

## Keywords

> Accurate
> Drop-down lists
> If statements
> Realistic

## Resources required

 **Whole Class Presentation: Unit 3.2**

 **Written Task: Checking a model**
**Written Task: Checking a model (Suggested answers)**

 **Interactive Test: Interpreting a spreadsheet model**

 **End of Unit Activity 3.2: Developing the mobile phone model (L4–5)**
**End of Unit Activity 3.2: Developing the mobile phone model (L5–6)**
**Mobile phone model (L4–5 only)**
**Mobile phone model (Suggested solution)**

 **Skills Tutorials 1–2**

**Pages 54–5 of the Pupil's Book**

## Teaching notes

1 Use the Module 3 Case Study to introduce pupils to the ways in which modelling is used in real situations, if necessary.
2 Use the Whole Class Presentation to explain the objectives of this unit and provide an overview of the main concept of improving the accuracy and realism of computer models.
3 Explain how models are only useful if they recreate real-life situations in an accurate and realistic way. Give examples. Use the 'Concert Hall Evacuation' model as an example.
4 Show how the 'Concert Hall Evacuation' model was developed to make it more realistic. Use pages 54–5 of the Pupil's Book. Explain drop-down lists and If statements.
5 Pupils complete the Interactive Test.
6 Pupils complete the Written Task 'Checking a model' to suggest changes that could be made to the 'Mobile Phone' model.
7 Pupils complete the End of Unit Activity 'Developing the mobile phone model' to put these changes into practice. Pupils may need to work through the Skills Tutorials.

## Assessment guidance for End of Unit Activity

**L4** Pupils use ICT-based models and simulations to explore patterns and relationships and make predictions about the consequences of their decisions.

Pupils should be able to take the model given to them and create a working solution. It may lack efficiency and may not be accurate in terms of what would happen in real life, but they should be able to enter formulae that work.

**L5** Pupils explore the effects of changing the variables in an ICT-based model.

Pupils develop the model to improve the accuracy. They should take account of the suggestions they made in the earlier written task about how to improve the model, and implement some of those changes.

**L6** Pupils use ICT-based models to make predictions and vary the rules within the models. They assess the validity of these models by comparing their behaviour with information from other sources.

Pupils should be able to create the model from scratch largely unaided. They test that the model works correctly and check it against real data. You would expect to see the use of efficient tools such as If statements and the use of drop-down lists. They should implement improvements to the model.

# 3.3 | Teacher's Notes
## Using graphs to model data

## Lesson objectives

This unit develops the work that pupils did on graphing data in Unit 3.7 in InteraCT 1. Pupils look at how data needs to be set up in a suitable format to allow meaningful graphs to be created. They adapt the 'Concert hall evacuation' model into a table format so that it can be plotted. They use a graph of the data to answer 'what if' questions. They use graphs as a way of analysing information rather than simply as a way of presenting information.

Pupils extend their skills with spreadsheets using absolute cell references and graphing over non-contiguous cells.

## PoS reference

2.2a) select and use ICT tools and techniques appropriately, safely and efficiently.
2.2b) solve problems by developing, exploring and structuring information, and deriving new information for a particular purpose.
2.2c) test predictions and discover patterns and relationships, exploring, evaluating and developing models by changing their rules and values.
3a) use a range of information, with different characteristics, structures and purposes, and evaluation of how it matches requirements and its fitness for purpose.

## Framework reference

Finding things out:

> Organising and investigating: explore and interpret collected data in order to draw conclusions

Developing ideas and making things happen:

> Models and modelling: develop ICT-based models and test predictions; draw and explain conclusions; improve the accuracy and extend the scope of ICT models

## STU reference

8.4

## A&A CD-ROM reference

Strand M Activities 1–4
**InteraCT 1 Ref:** Module 3

## PLTS

Independent enquirer
Reflective learner

## Every Child Matters

Enjoy and achieve
Achieve economic well-being

## Differentiation and inclusion

Levelled worksheets in the Unit Assessment
Opportunities for peer- and self-review

## Keywords

> Absolute cell reference
> Relative cell reference
> Table
> Text labels

## Resources required

**Whole Class Presentation: Unit 3.3**

**Written Task: Setting up data**
**Written Task: Setting up data (Suggested answers)**
**Science experiment spreadsheet results (Suggested solution)**

**Interactive Test: Data and graphs**

**End of Unit Activity 3.3: Graphing data (L4–5)**
**End of Unit Activity 3.3: Graphing data (L5–6)**
**End of Unit Activity 3.3: Graphing data (L4–5 Suggested graphs and answers)**
**End of Unit Activity 3.3: Graphing data (L5–6 Suggested graphs and answers)**
**Running times spreadsheet (Suggested solution)**

**Skills Tutorial 1**

**Pages 56–7 of the Pupil's Book**

## Teaching notes

1 Use the Module 3 Case Study to introduce pupils to the ways in which modelling is used in real situations, if necessary.

2 Use the Whole Class Presentation to explain the objectives of this unit and provide an overview of the main concept of using graphs for modelling.

3 Explain how data needs to be set out in a certain way to allow meaningful graphs to be created. Use the 'Concert Hall Extended' model as an example. There are two worksheets showing the original model and the tabulated data.

4 Show how the 'Concert Hall Evacuation' model was developed to make it more realistic. Use pages 56–7 of the Pupil's Book. Explain drop-down lists and If statements.

5 Pupils complete the 'Setting up data' worksheet (Written Task), which they can do as a written or practical exercise.

6 Demonstrate to pupils how they can read data from a graph. Use the examples on page 57 of the Pupil's Book.

7 Pupils complete the Interactive Test.

8 Pupils may need to work through the Skills Tutorial at this stage to see how to set up data in a table, use an absolute reference and plot non-contiguous cells of data.

9 Pupils complete the End of Unit Activity 'Graphing data'.

## Assessment guidance for End of Unit Activity

**L4** Pupils use ICT to structure, refine and present information in different forms and styles for specific purposes and audiences. They use ICT to organise, store and retrieve information using logical and appropriate structures.

They may need considerable help in graphing the appropriate data and finding the answers to the questions.

**L5** Pupils use ICT to structure, refine and present information in different forms and styles for specific purposes and audiences.

They are able to answer most of the questions, though they may need some help initially to create the graphs and charts needed. Once they have been shown how to create one graph, they should be able to create a comparable graph and find the information they need.

**L6** Pupils plan and design ICT-based solutions to meet a specific purpose and audience, demonstrating increased integration and efficiency in their use of ICT tools. They develop and refine their work to enhance its quality, using a greater range and complexity of information. Where necessary, they use complex lines of enquiry to test hypotheses. They present their ideas in a variety of ways and show a clear sense of audience.

Pupils work largely unaided creating suitable graphs in order to find the information they need. They should be able to answer all the questions correctly based on the graphs they have produced. They should present the graphs in the answer sheet as evidence.

# 3.4 Teacher's Notes
## Using simulations

## Lesson objectives

This unit focuses on the use of simulations to make predictions about real life. Pupils are introduced to the concept of simulations as the output from a computer model. Analogies are drawn to computer games, many of which are simulations.

Pupils are reminded that models are built from variables and rules, and pupils are asked to consider how variables and rules might be used within simulations.

Pupils are shown and then use the Investment Manager model, which predicts what might happen to an investment of £10,000. Teachers should familiarise themselves with the model before starting the unit. Pupils may need some guidance on the financial terms involved, although they have been kept relatively straightforward. Gambling is mentioned as a possible 'investment' option so teachers may want to discuss the wider implications of this.

## PoS reference

2.2c) test predictions and discover patterns and relationships, exploring, evaluating and developing models by changing their rules and values.
2.4c) reflect on what they have learnt and use these insights to improve future work.

## Framework reference

Finding things out:

> Organising and investigating: explore and interpret collected data in order to draw conclusions

Developing ideas and making things happen:

> Models and modelling: develop ICT-based models and test predictions; draw and explain conclusions; improve the accuracy and extend the scope of ICT models

## STU reference

8.4

## A&A CD-ROM reference

Strand M Activities 1–4
**InteraCT 1 Ref:** Module 3

## PLTS

Independent enquirer
Reflective learner
Creative thinker

## Every Child Matters

Enjoy and achieve
Achieve economic well-being

## Differentiation and inclusion

Levelled worksheets in the Unit Assessment

## Keywords

> Investment
> Real-life
> Rules
> Simulation
> Variables

## Resources required

 **Whole Class Presentation: Unit 3.4**

 **Written Task: Variables and Rules**
**Written Task: Variables and Rules (Suggested answers)**

 **Interactive Test: Variables and rules**

 **End of Unit Activity 3.4: Understanding Investment Manager (L4–5)**
**End of Unit Activity 3.4: Understanding Investment Manager (L5–6)**
**End of Unit Activity 3.4: Understanding Investment Manager (Suggested answers)**

 **Skills Tutorial 1**

 **Investment Manager spreadsheet**

**Pages 58–61 of the Pupil's Book**

## Teaching notes

1 Use the Module 3 Case Study to introduce pupils to the ways in which modelling is used in real situations, if necessary.
2 Use the Whole Class Presentation to explain the objectives of this unit and provide an overview of simulations.
3 Discuss the concept of simulations. Ask pupils for examples for computer games they have played with a real-world context.
4 Re-visit the concept of variables and explain the rules. Discuss some of the variables and rules that they might find in typical simulation games.
5 Pupils complete the Written Task 'Variables and rules'.
6 Explain that simulations can also be created in Excel. Introduce the 'Investment Manager' spreadsheet. Demonstrate it in some detail.
7 Pupils complete the Interactive Test.
8 Pupils may need to work through the Skills Tutorial at this stage, to see how to interact with the 'Investment Manager' model.
9 Pupils complete the End of Unit Activity 'Understanding Investment Manager'.

## Assessment guidance for End of Unit Activity

**L4** Pupils use ICT-based models and simulations to explore patterns and relationships, and make predictions about the consequences of their decisions.
   They may type in fairly random selections until they get the best and worst results. There may be little purpose to this but, over a period of time, they may arrive at the correct solutions. Typically, they rely on trial and error.

**L5** Pupils explore the effects of changing the variables in an ICT-based model.
   They should demonstrate slightly more purpose in terms of arriving at a result and show some understanding of the underlying rules. For example, they work out exactly what will produce the best and worst results.

**L6** Pupils use ICT-based models to make predictions and vary the rules within the models. They assess the validity of these models by comparing their behaviour with information from other sources.
   They should be able to use the model and demonstrate their understanding of it by answering all the questions correctly. The last three questions are designed specifically to demonstrate L6 capability and sensible answers to the final question would be a good indication of a pupil working at L6.

# 3.5 Teacher's Notes
## Creating a simulation

## Lesson objectives

This unit follows on from where Unit 3.4 left off. Pupils create their own model and simulation. They are shown how to create a model to simulate a game where two dice are thrown and the results are added together (a variation on Craps). This introduces them to the use of random numbers.

Pupils are also shown conditional formatting and If statements, which are a useful way of adding usability to spreadsheet models. In this case, the cells change colour when someone 'wins' and a statement is generated in one of the cells to tell players whether they have won or not.

## PoS reference

2.2c) test predictions and discover patterns and relationships, exploring, evaluating and developing models by changing their rules and values.
2.4c) reflect on what they have learnt and use these insights to improve future work.

## Framework reference

Finding things out:

> Organising and investigating: explore and interpret collected data in order to draw conclusions

Developing ideas and making things happen:

> Models and modelling: develop ICT-based models and test predictions; draw and explain conclusions; improve the accuracy and extend the scope of ICT models

## STU reference

8.4

## A&A CD-ROM reference

Strand M Activities 1–4
**InteraCT 1 Ref:** Module 3

## PLTS

Independent enquirer
Reflective learner
Creative thinker

## Every Child Matters

Enjoy and achieve
Achieve economic well-being

## Differentiation and inclusion

Levelled worksheets in the Unit Assessment

## Keywords

> Conditional formatting
> Nested If statement
> RANDBETWEEN
> Random numbers

## Resources required

 **Whole Class Presentation: Unit 3.5**

 **Written Task: Random numbers**
**Written Task: Random numbers (Answers)**

 **Interactive Test: Setting up a simulation**

 **End of Unit Activity 3.5: Card game simulation (L4–5)**
**End of Unit Activity 3.5: Card game simulation (L5–6)**

 **End of Unit Activity 3.5: Card game simulation (Suggested answers)**
**Card game simulation spreadsheet (L4/5 only)**
**Card game simulation spreadsheet (Suggested solution)**

**Skills Tutorials 1–3**

 **National Lottery simulation spreadsheet**
**The dice game spreadsheet**
**Dartboard simulation spreadsheet**

**Pages 62–3 of the Pupil's Book**

## Teaching notes

1 Use the Module 3 Case Study to introduce pupils to the ways in which modelling is used in real situations, if necessary.
2 Use the Whole Class Presentation to explain the objectives of this unit.
3 Explain the dice game to the pupils. You could demonstrate it and allow pupils to play with the 'Dice Game' model. Show pupils how the random numbers are generated every time F9 is pressed.
4 Explain the concept of random numbers and how they can be used to create the uncertainty of real life, e.g. there is a 1 in 6 chance of throwing any of the numbers.
5 Pupils complete the 'Random numbers' worksheet (Written task).
6 The Skills Tutorials can be triggered from any one of three points depending on which stage you want them to try it for themselves.
7 Explain the concept of conditional formatting. Demonstrate it using the 'Dice Game' model.
8 Demonstrate If statements. Explain to pupils that this is a slightly more complex If statement than the ones they have done so far in this unit: one If statement is nested inside another If statement.
9 Pupils complete the Interactive Test.
10 Pupils complete the End of Unit Activity 'Card game simulation'. Pupils can work through the Skills Tutorials at this stage if they have not done so already.
11 Pupils complete the End of Module Assignment.

## Assessment guidance for End of Unit Activity

**L4** Pupils use ICT-based models and simulations to explore patterns and relationships, and make predictions about the consequences of their decisions.
They should be given the 'Card game simulation' spreadsheet to work on as they would find it difficult to create it from scratch. They may need guidance in creating the first random number, but should be able to create the other two after that. They should then create a formula to add the 3 cards together.

**L5** Pupils explore the effects of changing the variables in an ICT-based model.
They should be able to create the formulae for the random numbers and the sum of the cards using the template provided. They should be able to add conditional formatting but may find the If statement difficult. The suggested solution provided is a typical L5 response.

**L6** Pupils use ICT-based models to make predictions and vary the rules within the models. They assess the validity of these models by comparing their behaviour with information from other sources.
They should be able to create a model from scratch and use formulae to create the random numbers and the total. They should be able to create an If statement. Their simulation should be an accurate representation of the card game in real life.

# 4 Teacher's Notes
## Data handling

## Module structure

Data handling was covered in InteraCT 1 and this module aims to extend and develop pupils' capabilities beyond the basics. The module focuses on creating databases from scratch using database software. Pupils create database structures and go on to create forms for viewing and entering data. Pupils are introduced to the concept of queries and consider the ways that data can be presented, including integrating it into other software.

This module uses Microsoft Access although all aspects of the units (apart from the Skills Tutorials) can be used with any database software.

Unit 4.1 focuses on setting up the database: selecting the appropriate data types, field lengths and validation. Unit 4.2 is specifically about using forms to view and enter data held on a database. Pupils also consider the use of online forms. Unit 4.3 focuses on querying a database and in Unit 4.4 pupils consider ways in which information from a database can be presented.

As with all the modules, there are some module resources that you can use before you start on the units. These are:

> Module 4 Case Study
> Module 4 Starter Activities

## Assessment

Most assessments in this module are designed to allow pupils to demonstrate levels 4 to 6. There are levelled Unit Assessments and interpretation of the levels is provided in the Teacher's Notes for each unit.

There is also a levelled Module Assignment that pupils can work on when all the units are complete. This is designed to cover all aspects of this module. This is a differentiated activity and you should give each pupil the worksheet that is most appropriate to the level that you think they are working towards. The interpretation of levels for the Module Assignment is given below.

## Assessment guidance for Module Assignment

Please note that there is a suggested answers document on the CD-ROM.

**L4** Pupils understand the need for care in framing questions when collecting, finding and interrogating information. They use ICT to organise, store and retrieve information.

They should be able to recognise that badly worded questions lead to poor results. They should be able to ask and structure some questions that elicit the information needed. They should be able to choose the most appropriate data types for most questions with little or no guidance.

Pupils should be able to create a form largely unaided. Their finished form should demonstrate some consistency in terms of the overall layout. Fonts should be used consistently and questions should be numbered. They should add a title and make good use of the space on the page. The work should be spell-checked.

Pupils may answer the final question in a fairly cursory way without fully explaining how datasets can be searched or sorted.

**L5** Pupils select the information they need for different purposes, check its accuracy and organise

it in a form suitable for processing. They use ICT to organise, store and retrieve information using logical and appropriate structures.

They should be able to identify what data is needed and create the database form largely unaided, selecting suitable questions with the most appropriate data type in each case. They may need prompting to add validation checks.

They should sequence fields in a logical order with similar questions grouped together. They may divide the form in some way to indicate this. They may add information helpful to the user such as a heading or instructions on what each field is.

Pupils should identify that databases can be searched or sorted to find answers.

**L6** Pupils develop and refine their work to enhance its quality, using a greater range and complexity of information.

They set up the database completely unaided, creating a suitable database table and form. They go on to explain in detail how the database could be interrogated to provide the information that the school needs. They discuss some of the wider uses of the data that have been collected.

# Suggested answers to questions posed in the Case Study

Q What information do you think AgeProof are going to need before they can issue an ID card? Where will they get this information?

**Suggested answers:**
> Full name
> Full address
> Postcode
> Email address
> Telephone number
> Date of birth
> Gender
> Today's date
> A photograph
> Proof from a parent or guardian
> Parent's or guardian's name

This information will be collected from the applicants and their parents or guardians.

Q What problems might there be with this way of getting the forms filled in? How could they solve these problems?

**Suggested answers:**
> It will take time for the person to receive the form, fill it in and then post it back.
> The attachment may not download correctly.
> The applicant could make errors on the form.
> The person at AgeProof might make errors as they type the data into the computer.

They could solve these problems by having an online form that is as easy to fill in as possible.

Q What fields do they need to store? What data types should they use for each field? What validation checks should there be on each field?

| Field name | Data type | Validation |
|---|---|---|
| First Name | Text | Length check 30 characters/Presence check |
| Last Name | Text | Length check 50 characters/Presence check |
| Address | Text | Presence check |
| Postcode | Text | Format check TTNN NTT/Presence check |
| Date of Birth | DOB | Format check NN/NN/NNNN |
| Gender | M/C | Male/Female |
| Email address | Text | None |

Pupils may identify other fields relevant to an application, such as parent's name, whether proof of age has been sent, etc.

Q What problems might there be in asking people to fill in their data on this screen?

**Suggested answers:**
> Some boxes are too small for the answers.
> Some of the labels are not long enough to let you read what is needed in the answer space.
> The layout does not make it easy to fill in.
> There are no instructions and no title so people won't know what it is.

Q What improvements do you think could be made to this form?

**Suggested answers:**
> Lay it out neatly making better use of the space.
> Increase the size of the answer spaces.
> Make sure that the labels are big enough to be able to read what information is needed.
> Add a title and some instructions on how to fill the form in.

Q How else could AgeProof use the information stored in the database?

**Suggested answers:**
They could analyse the data to help them understand more about the people who are applying for cards. For example, they could look at the average age of people applying or whether more females or males apply for cards.

Q How could AgeProof use the database to find out this information? How could they present this information?

**Suggested answers:**
They would have to search and/or sort the database. They could present the information as a table or a graph.

Q How else could this information have been presented to the managers at AgeProof?

**Suggested answers:**
It could have been presented as:

> a slideshow presentation
> a DTP publication (e.g. a leaflet or newsletter)
> a web page.

# 4.1 Teacher's Notes
## Setting up a database

## Lesson objectives

Data handling was covered in InteraCT 1 but this is the first time pupils have come across database software. The unit starts with a brief reminder of the main aspects of data handling and databases and many of the keywords are revisited.

Pupils set up a database from scratch, using a table in Access. This involves the selection of suitable data types and field lengths for storing the data. Pupils go on to consider suitable validation checks.

These topics were covered in InteraCT 1, so this will consolidate pupils' knowledge. The main difference here is that pupils go on to set up a database from scratch using a database package.

It is possible to complete all of the tasks in this unit using any database software although the Skills Tutorials only show pupils how to use Access.

## PoS reference

2.1a) consider systematically the information needed to solve a problem, complete a task or answer a question, and explore how it will be used.
2.1c) collect and enter quantitative and qualitative information, checking its accuracy.
2.2b) solve problems by developing, exploring and structuring information, and deriving new information for a particular purpose.
2.2d) design information systems and suggest improvements to existing systems.

## Framework reference

Finding things out:

> Organising and investigating: store, retrieve and present electronic material efficiently

## STU reference

7.5

## A&A CD-ROM reference

Strand DH Activities 1–4

## PLTS

Independent enquirer
Reflective learner
Creative thinker

## Every Child Matters

Enjoy and achieve
Achieve economic well-being

## Differentiation and inclusion

Levelled worksheets in the Unit Assessment

## Keywords

> Data capture
> Data collection
> Data structure
> Database software
> Field length
> Field size
> Form
> Online form
> Police National Computer database
> Query
> Table

# Resources required

 **Whole Class Presentation: Unit 4.1**

 **Written Task: Designing a data structure**
**Written Task: Designing a data structure (Suggested answers)**

 **Interactive Test: Data handling**

 **End of Unit Activity 4.1: Setting up a database**

 **Skills Tutorials 1–2**

 **Car insurance database**
**Example database**

**Pages 68–9 of the Pupil's Book**

# Teaching notes

1 Use the Module 4 Case Study to introduce pupils to the ways in which modelling is used in real situations.
2 Use the Whole Class Presentation to explain the objectives of this unit.
3 Consolidate previous learning on data handling and databases from InteraCT 1. Recap on the definition of a database with examples of uses.
4 Pupils complete the Interactive Test, which acts as a reminder of the key aspects of data handling.
5 Explain the concepts of data collection and data capture.
6 Remind pupils about data types, field lengths and validation.
7 Pupils complete the 'Designing a data structure' worksheet (Written Task).
8 Introduce Microsoft Access. You should demonstrate how to make a table.
9 Pupils complete the End of Unit Activity 'Setting up a database'. They may need to use the Skills Tutorials if they are doing this in Access.

# Assessment guidance for End of Unit Activity

The process of setting up the structure for a database and then creating a form have been split over Units 4.1 and 4.2. A more accurate level can be given to pupils by assessing the combined results of the two activities. Therefore, you may choose to assess the activities of Units 4.1 and 4.2 as if they were one assignment. These activities allow pupils to demonstrate capability at L4 and L5. More detailed analysis of a dataset is needed to achieve L6.

**L4** Pupils understand the need for care in framing questions when collecting, finding and interrogating information. They use ICT to organise, store and retrieve information.
  Pupils should be able to recognise that badly worded questions lead to poor results. They should be able to ask and structure questions that will elicit the information needed. They should be able to choose the most appropriate data types with little or no guidance.

**L5** Pupils select the information they need for different purposes, check its accuracy and organise it in a form suitable for processing. They use ICT to organise, store and retrieve information using logical and appropriate structures.
  They should be able to identify what data is needed and create the database form largely unaided, selecting suitable questions with the most appropriate data type in each case. They may need prompting to add validation checks.

DL DYNAMIC LEARNING © Hodder Education 2008

# 4.2

## Teacher's Notes
## Working with forms

## Lesson objectives

This unit follows on directly from Unit 4.1. Pupils look at forms and learn how to create a form to use with the databases that they have set up. Parallels are drawn with the questionnaire design that pupils did in InteraCT 1.

The use of forms is explored in terms of how they can be used to enter data and to view data that is already in a database. The use of online forms is also covered.

It is possible to complete all of the tasks in this unit using any database software although the Skills Tutorial only shows pupils how to use Access.

## PoS reference

2.2a) select and use ICT tools and techniques appropriately, safely and efficiently.
2.2d) design information systems and suggest improvements to existing systems.

## Framework reference

Finding things out:

> Organising and investigating: store, retrieve and present electronic material efficiently

Developing ideas and making things happen:

> Analysing and automating processes: automate simple processes

## STU reference

7.5

## A&A CD-ROM reference

Strand DH Activities 1–4

## PLTS

Independent enquirer
Reflective learner
Creative thinker

## Every Child Matters

Enjoy and achieve
Achieve economic well-being

## Differentiation and inclusion

Levelled worksheets in the Unit Assessment

## Keywords

> Computer-based forms
> Drop-down lists
> Online forms
> Paper-based forms
> Tick boxes
> User-friendly

# Resources required

 **Whole Class presentation: Unit 4.2**

 **Written Task: Designing a form**
**Written Task: Designing a form (Suggested answers)**

 **Interactive Test: Databases: forms**

 **End of Unit Activity 4.2: Setting up a form**

 **Skills Tutorial 1**

 **Car insurance database**

**Pages 70–1 of the Pupil's Book**

# Teaching notes

1 Use the Module 4 Case Study to introduce pupils to the ways in which modelling is used in real situations.
2 Use the Whole Class Presentation to explain the objectives of this unit.
3 Introduce the concept of a form for entering and viewing data in a database. Draw parallels with questionnaires. Show the data as a table and as a form (page 70 of the Pupil's Book) to illustrate the point.
4 Pupils complete the Interactive Test.
5 Explain where forms are used and point out some of the features of good design.
6 Pupils complete the Written Task 'Designing a form'.
7 Demonstrate how to make a form in Access (or your chosen software).
8 Pupils complete the End of Unit Activity 'Setting up a form'. They may need to use the Skills Tutorial if they are doing this in Access.

# Assessment guidance for End of Unit Activity

**L4** Pupils use ICT to organise, store and retrieve information.

In combination with the table that pupils created in Unit 4.1, pupils should be able to create a form largely unaided. Their finished form should demonstrate some consistency in terms of the overall layout. Fonts should be used consistently and questions should be numbered. The pupil should add a title. They should have made good use of the space on the page. The work should be spell-checked.

**L5** Pupils use ICT to organise, store and retrieve information using logical and appropriate structures.

Fields should be sequenced in a logical order with similar questions grouped together. They may divide the form into sections in some way to indicate this. They may add information helpful to the user, such as a heading or instructions on what each field is. The finished form should look professional, be entirely consistent and contain no errors.

DYNAMIC LEARNING © Hodder Education 2008

# 4.3 | Teacher's Notes
## Advanced search techniques

## Lesson objectives

This unit focuses on searching databases. The unit starts with an explanation of what a query is (a database search), drawing parallels with the data-handling work they did in InteraCT 1. Pupils go on to look at how a query is created by selecting a field or fields and then the criteria on which to search.

Pupils are shown some simple queries using one criterion and some more complex queries using several fields and criteria. There is also an explanation of some of the operators that pupils can use (=, >, <, <= , >= and BETWEEN).

Pupils use a small database of 50 records, which is used by a dog rescue charity to keep track of all of the dogs in their care. Pupils see how the database can be used in a purposeful way by an organisation. The database is provided as an Access database and also as a CSV file so that you can import it into a different database package if required.

## PoS reference

2.1a) consider systematically the information needed to solve a problem, complete a task or answer a question, and explore how it will be used.

2.1b) use and refine search methods to obtain information that is well matched to purpose, by selecting appropriate sources.

2.1d) analyse and evaluate information, judging its value, accuracy, plausibility and bias.

2.2a) select and use ICT tools and techniques appropriately, safely and efficiently.

2.2b) solve problems by developing, exploring and structuring information, and deriving new information for a particular purpose.

2.4c) reflect on what they have learnt and use these insights to improve future work.

## Framework reference

Finding things out:

> Searching and selecting: extend and refine search methods to be more efficient
> Organising and investigating: store, retrieve and present electronic material efficiently; explore and interpret collected data in order to draw conclusions; understand the impact of electronic databases on commercial practice and society

## STU reference

7.5

## A&A CD-ROM reference

Strand DH Activities 1–4

## PLTS

Independent enquirer
Reflective learner
Creative thinker

## Every Child Matters

Enjoy and achieve
Achieve economic well-being

## Differentiation and inclusion

Levelled worksheets in the Unit Assessment

## Keywords

> BETWEEN
> Complex query
> Criteria
> Criterion
> Greater than
> Greater than or equal to
> Less than
> Less than or equal to
> Query
> Simple query

**Whole Class Presentation: Unit 4.3**

 **Written Task: Writing queries**
**Written Task: Writing queries (Answers)**

 **Interactive Test: Queries**

 **End of Unit Activity 4.3: Querying the Dog Rescue database (L4–5)**
**End of Unit Activity 4.3: Querying the Dog Rescue database (L5–6)**

**Dog Rescue database**
**CSV version of the Dog Rescue database**
**End of Unit Activity 4.3: Querying the Dog Rescue database (L4–5 Answers)**
**End of Unit Activity 4.3: Querying the Dog Rescue database (L5–6 answers)**

 **Skills Tutorial 1**

**Pages 72–5 of the Pupil's Book**

## Teaching notes

1 Use the Module 4 Case Study to introduce pupils to the ways in which modelling is used in real situations.
2 Use the Whole Class Presentation to explain the objectives of this unit.
3 Show the 'Dog Rescue' database and give examples of typical queries that could be done. Explain the real-life use of queries in this context in terms of matching dogs to potential owners.
4 Pupils complete the Written Task 'Writing queries'.
5 Explain simple and complex queries including the use of AND and OR statements and the mathematical operators.
6 Pupils complete the Interactive Test.
7 Demonstrate how to query in Access (or your chosen software).
8 Pupils complete the End of Unit Activity 'Querying the Dog Rescue database'. They may need to use the Skills Tutorial if they are doing this in Access.

## Assessment guidance for End of Unit Activity

**L4** Pupils understand the need for care in framing questions when collecting, finding and interrogating information. They use ICT to organise, store and retrieve information.

They should be able to carry out simple sorts and queries largely unaided, perhaps requiring some guidance in the early stages. They should be able to carry out slightly more sophisticated queries using 'greater than' and 'less than'. They should be able to carry out a more complex query using two criteria and a single AND or OR operator.

Questions 1 to 5 of the L4/5 worksheet are designed for pupils working at L4.

**L5** Pupils select the information they need for different purposes, check its accuracy and organise it in a form suitable for processing. They use ICT to organise, store and retrieve information using logical and appropriate structures.

They should be able to carry out complex queries, combining them with sorts as required. They are able to work with two or three criteria and combine AND or OR operators as required.

Questions 6 to 10 of the L4/5 worksheet (which are the same as questions 1 to 5 of the L5/6 worksheet) are designed for pupils working at L5.

**L6** Pupils use complex lines of enquiry, where necessary, to test hypotheses.

They should be able to carry out complex queries, combining them with sorts as required. They are able to work with two or three criteria and combine AND or OR operators as required. They can test hypotheses by constructing queries and comparing the results of different queries. They may create queries from existing queries, demonstrating efficiency. They should also be able to make hypotheses by examining the data and the range of values within them. Having made a hypothesis, they can test it and explain their answers.

Questions 6 to 10 of the L5/6 worksheet are designed for pupils working at L6 as they have to interpret the question in order to work out what queries are needed.

# 4.4 Teacher's Notes
## Presenting results

## Lesson objectives

This unit focuses on the ways that data stored in a database can be presented. The standard way of viewing data in a database is in the form of a table and pupils are already familiar with this as a way of viewing the results of queries.

This unit looks at how the data can be put into a report. The advantages of using a report format are explained and pupils are asked to design reports for different scenarios. The Skills Tutorial shows how to create reports in Access from tables of data, including queries.

The concept of integrating the data with other software is also covered. In particular, pupils are asked to consider the purpose and audience and then to copy and paste the appropriate data into the appropriate software in order to present the results.

## PoS reference

2.1a) consider systematically the information needed to solve a problem, complete a task or answer a question, and explore how it will be used.
2.1b) use and refine search methods to obtain information that is well matched to purpose, by selecting appropriate sources.
2.1d) analyse and evaluate information, judging its value, accuracy, plausibility and bias.
2.2b) solve problems by developing, exploring and structuring information, and deriving new information for a particular purpose.
2.2f) bring together, draft and refine information, including through the combination of text, sound and image.
2.3a) use a range of ICT tools to present information in forms that are fit for purpose, meet audience needs and suit the content.
3a) use a range of information, with different characteristics, structures and purposes, and evaluation of how it matches requirements and its fitness for purpose.
3b) use a variety of information sources, including large data sets, in a range of contexts.
3c) use and review of the effectiveness of different ICT tools, including a range of software applications, in terms of meeting user needs and solving problems.

## Framework reference

Finding things out:

> Using data and information sources: understand how the content and style of an information source affect its suitability for particular purposes
> Searching and selecting: extend and refine search methods to be more efficient
> Organising and investigating: store, retrieve and present electronic material efficiently; explore and interpret collected data in order to draw conclusions

## STU reference

7.5

## A&A CD-ROM reference

Strand DH Activities 1–4

## PLTS

Independent enquirer
Reflective learner
Creative thinker

## Every Child Matters

Enjoy and achieve
Achieve economic well-being

## Differentiation and inclusion

Levelled worksheets in the Unit Assessment
Opportunities for peer and self review

## Keywords

> Columnar
> Integrated
> Integrating
> Report
> Report heading
> Tabular

## Resources required

 **Whole Class Presentation: Unit 4.4**

 **Interactive Test: Formatting a database report**

 **Skills Tutorial 1**

 **Film database**
**Dog rescue database**

 **Written Task: Designing a report**
**Written Task: Designing a report (Suggested answers)**

 **Practical Task: Creating a report**
**Practical Task: Creating a report (Suggested answers)**
**End of Unit Activity 4.4: Presenting the results (L4–5)**
**End of Unit Activity 4.4: Presenting the results (L5–6)**
**Pages 76–9 of the Pupil's Book**

## Teaching notes

1 Use the Module 4 Case Study to introduce pupils to the ways in which modelling is used in real situations.
2 Use the Whole Class Presentation to explain the objectives of this unit.
3 Remind pupils that databases exist because people need to get information out of them. Explain how data are stored as a table. Explain how this might not always be the most appropriate way of viewing the data.
4 Demonstrate how to create a report in database software.
5 Pupils complete the Interactive Test.
6 If using Access, pupils should complete the Skills Tutorial now.
7 Pupils complete the Written Task 'Designing a report' and the Practical Task 'Creating a report'. In this unit, the two tasks are related. The Written Task gets the pupils to plan a design and the Practical Task gets them to carry it out. You may choose to do either or both.
8 Explain how data can be integrated across different software. Use the PowerPoint example on page 78 of the Pupil's Book.
9 Pupils complete the End of Unit Activity 'Presenting the results'.
10 Pupils complete the End of Module Assignment.

## Assessment guidance for End of Unit Activity

**L4** In addition to the criteria given in the first paragraph under L4 in Unit 1.2, pupils use ICT to present information in different forms and show they are aware of the intended audience and the need for quality in their presentations. They exchange information and ideas with others in a variety of ways, including using digital communication. Pupils interrogate the database to get useful information for their presentations. This may be through a single search or sort. They may need some guidance in identifying what information would be useful for the stated purpose. They create a table or graph of the data or just take raw figures from the dataset. They copy and paste this into some form of presentation. The presentation shows some awareness of the purpose and the audience.

**L5** In addition to the criteria given in the first paragraph for L5 in Unit 1.2, pupils combine ICT tools within the overall structure of an ICT solution. They exchange information and ideas with others in a variety of ways, including using digital communications. Pupils need little guidance in finding information that is suitable for their purpose. They do this through a series of queries on the database. Typically this might include fairly complex searches using multiple criteria. The finished presentation shows a clear sense of purpose and audience.

**L6** In addition to the criteria given in the first sentence for L6 in Unit 1.2, pupils plan and design ICT-based solutions to meet a specific purpose and audience, demonstrating increased integration and efficiency in their use of ICT tools. They present their ideas in a variety of ways and show a clear sense of audience.

The L5/6 worksheet is deliberately open-ended, and it is a characteristic of pupils working at L6 that they interpret this for themselves, selecting the most appropriate information and ICT tools to create a presentation that is suitable for the purpose and the audience.

They may include complex searches on the database that elicit information that supports the cause of the dog rescue service. The finished presentation could be in any form, e.g. presentation, DTP publication or word-processed document, and shows a very clear sense of purpose and audience.

# 5 Teacher's Notes
## Control

## Module structure

Control was covered in InteraCT 1 and this module aims to extend and develop pupils' capabilities beyond the basics. The module focuses on pupils creating sequences of instructions and flowcharts from scratch, aiming for precision and efficiency in their results. There are no new skills to learn.

5.1 Creating sets of instructions to control events
5.2 Making control instructions more precise
5.3 Making control instructions more efficient
5.4 Monitoring and control systems

Unit 5.1 aims to consolidate pupils' learning from InteraCT 1 and to create a flowchart from scratch. Unit 5.2 focuses on the need to create precise instructions. Pupils look at examples of flowcharts that are correct but not precise, with a view to improving the accuracy of their work. Unit 5.3 is concerned with efficiency, which is a feature of higher-level ICT capability. Loops, subroutines and variables are re-visited and pupils build them into their flowchart solutions.

As with all the modules, there are some module resources that you can use before you start on the units. These are:

> Module 5 Case Study
> Module 5 Starter Activities

## Assessment

All assessments in this module are designed to allow pupils to demonstrate levels 4 to 6. There are levelled Unit Assessments and interpretation of the levels is provided in the Teacher's Notes for each unit. There is also a levelled Module Assignment that pupils can work on when all the units are complete. This is designed to cover all aspects of this module. This is a differentiated activity and you should give each pupil the worksheet that is most appropriate to the level that you think they are working towards. The interpretation of levels for the Module Assignment is given below.

## Assessment guidance for Module Assignment

Typical solutions have been provided for L4/5 and L5/6.

**L4** Pupils plan and test sequences of instructions. They create a basic flowchart containing the main processes, although it may lack precision and efficiency. However, it should work.

**L5** Pupils create sequences of instructions and understand the need to be precise when framing and sequencing instructions.

They create a system that works and is quite precise, in that the processes are broken down into fairly detailed steps. However, it may lack

efficiency. For example, instructions may be repeated where perhaps a loop or subroutine could be used.

**L6** Pupils develop, try out and refine sequences of instructions and show efficiency in framing these instructions, using subroutines where appropriate.

They should provide an efficient and complete solution. The suggested answer shows a typical L6 solution that includes the use of a subroutine. You should also expect the pupil to fully annotate the flowchart to show a full understanding of what is happening at each stage.

# Suggested answers to questions posed in the Case Study

Q How could Lorna use ICT to help her with her drive into London?

**Suggested answers:**

Lorna could use:

> a satellite navigation system in her car
> traffic information provided on the satellite navigation system
> traffic information from websites (e.g. the AA or RAC) sent to her PDA or home computer
> traffic information sent by text message.

Q How does the satellite navigation system know where Lorna is? How could the system know if there was a traffic jam?

**Suggested answers:**

The satnav sends out a signal to the satellite which can then locate it using a grid reference.

The satnav uses information collected from satellites and roadside cameras. If there is no movement from the vehicles then there is a traffic jam and the system sends an alert to the satnav to tell the driver to go a different way.

Q How could computers be used to catch speeding drivers?

Speed cameras.

Q How does the speed camera work? How does the speed camera know whose car it is? How does the speed camera know who is driving?

**Suggested answers:**

The speed camera can use sensors to work out if a vehicle is travelling faster than the speed limit. If it is, the speed camera takes a digital photograph of the vehicle as it passes. This captures the car, the number plate, the date and time, and the speed.

The number plate links the car to the person that owns it. All this information is stored in a database (the DVLA database).

The speed camera does not know who is driving. It only knows who owns the vehicle and it is the owner who gets the speeding ticket.

Q How will the council know whether Lorna has driven into the congestion zone? How will the council know whether Lorna has paid or not?

**Suggested answers:**

Cameras are used to photograph the number plate of every vehicle that enters the congestion zone.

Lorna registers her number plate when she makes a payment. All this information is stored on a database. The system can check whether a payment has been made for that vehicle. If not, the vehicle is traced and the owner receives a fine notice.

Q What information might be stored on the swipe card? Why might some people not like the idea of being recorded on CCTV?

**Suggested answers:**

The swipe card contains some kind of code so that the system knows it is a valid card. It may also contain personal information about Lorna, such as her name and the registration number of her car. Some people might think it is an invasion of privacy to be filmed without being asked first. People might be worried about what happens to the recording and who will see it.

Q What computer systems has Lorna used today? Has it been useful for Lorna to use these systems? Are there any possible problems with using computer systems like these?

**Suggested answers:**

Lorna has used:

> a satellite navigation system
> her home computer and PDA
> a mobile phone
> a speed camera
> a congestion charge system
> a swipe-card, car-park-entry system
> a swipe-card, door-entry system
> a CCTV system.

In most cases, the computer systems Lorna has used have been useful to her:

> They may have reduced the time it took to get to work.
> They helped her avoid sitting in traffic jams.
> They have caught people speeding, which makes the road safer.
> They have kept her car and office safe from intruders.

In some cases, the computer systems might have been a bad thing for Lorna:

> She has had to pay a congestion charge.
> She has been recorded on CCTV, which she might not like.
> What would have happened if the computer systems had failed?

DL DYNAMIC LEARNING © Hodder Education 2008

# 5.1 Teacher's Notes
## Creating sets of instructions to control events

## Lesson objectives

Computer control was covered in InteraCT 1, so this first unit starts with a reminder of the basics. Pupils can start with the online test to see how much they recall. Pupils need to be reminded of the widespread use of computer-controlled devices and how they are controlled using instructions. The instructions can be represented in the form of a flowchart. Pupils may need to be reminded of the main flowchart symbols.

Pupils go through the process of working out the instructions that would be needed for a typical control application and turn them into a full flowchart. Pupils are asked to create a flowchart from scratch for themselves. There are no new software skills to learn in InteraCT 2, so the emphasis is on the creation of an accurate and efficient system.

## PoS reference

2.2e) use ICT to make things happen by planning, testing and modifying a sequence of instructions, recognising where a group of instructions needs repeating, and automating frequently used processes by constructing efficient procedures that are fit for purpose.
2.3c) use technical terms appropriately and correctly.
2.4b) reflect on their own and others' uses of ICT to help them develop and improve their ideas and the quality of their work.
2.4c) reflect on what they have learnt and use these insights to improve future work.

## Framework reference

Developing ideas and making things happen:

> Analysing and automating processes: automate simple processes; represent simple design specifications as diagrams
> Control and monitoring: develop and test a system to monitor and control events

## Resources required

**Whole Class Presentation: Unit 5.1**

**Written Task: Writing control instructions**
**Written Task: Writing control instructions (Suggested answer)**
**End of Unit Activity 5.1: Creating a flowchart**
**End of Unit Activity 5.1: Creating a flowchart (Suggested answer)**

**Interactive Test: Computer control**

**Pages 84–5 of the Pupil's Book**

## STU reference

8.1, 8.6

## A&A CD-ROM reference

Strand C Activities 1–3

## PLTS

Independent enquirer
Reflective learner

## Every Child Matters

Enjoy and achieve

## Differentiation and inclusion

Levelled worksheets in the Unit Assessment
Opportunities for peer- and self-review

## Keywords

> Bluetooth
> Chip
> Computer microchip
> Error messages
> Memory card
> Wireless connection

# Teaching notes

1 Use the Module 5 Case Study to introduce the module.
2 Use the Whole Class Presentation to explain the objectives of this unit and provide an overview.
3 Remind pupils of the widespread use of computer control systems, of how flowcharts can represent a control system and of the main flowcharting symbols.
4 Pupils complete the Interactive Test.
5 Work through the digital photograph machine example (pages 84–5 of the Pupil's Book). Explain how it has been broken down into steps. Explain how they should account for all possible actions, e.g. when the user does something that they shouldn't do.
6 Pupils complete the 'Writing control instructions' worksheet (WFT).
7 Show pupils the flowchart for the digital photograph machine (pages 84–5 of the Pupil's Book).
8 Pupils complete the End of Unit Activity 'Creating a flowchart'.

# Assessment guidance for End of Unit Activity

**L4** Pupils plan and test sequences of instructions.

They create a basic flowchart containing the main processes, although it may lack precision and efficiency. However, it should work.

**L5** Pupils create sequences of instructions and understand the need to be precise when framing and sequencing instructions.

A typical response is shown in the 'suggested answer' document. This shows a system that works and includes every process.

**L6** Pupils develop, try out and refine sequences of instructions and show efficiency in framing these instructions, using sub-routines where appropriate.

You are looking for an efficient and complete solution. For example, they may include other payment methods in the flowchart, which may necessitate the use of a subroutine. You would also expect them to annotate the flowchart to show a full understanding of what is happening at each stage.

# 5.2

## Teacher's Notes
## Making control instructions more precise

## Lesson objectives

The focus of this unit is for pupils to develop precision in their control solutions. Higher-level capability in control is demonstrated through the increased precision of control instructions. This means that pupils should break down solutions into smaller steps and take account of all possibilities.

Pupils are encouraged to think about problems that could occur in real life and to take account of them in their flowcharts. Pupils are shown that they must break the flowcharts down into smaller and smaller steps to ensure that they work correctly.

Pupils should aim for efficiency as well as precision. There is more on this in the next unit.

## PoS reference

2.2e) use ICT to make things happen by planning, testing and modifying a sequence of instructions, recognising where a group of instructions needs repeating, and automating frequently used processes by constructing efficient procedures that are fit for purpose.
2.3c) use technical terms appropriately and correctly.
2.4b) reflect on their own and others' uses of ICT to help them develop and improve their ideas and the quality of their work.
2.4c) reflect on what they have learnt and use these insights to improve future work.

## Framework reference

Developing ideas and making things happen:

> Analysing and automating processes: automate simple processes; represent simple design specifications as diagrams
> Control and monitoring: develop and test a system to monitor and control events

## STU reference

8.1, 8.6

## A&A CD-ROM reference

Strand C Activities 1–3

## PLTS

Independent enquirer
Reflective learner
Creative thinker

## Every Child Matters

Enjoy and achieve
Achieve economic well-being

## Differentiation and inclusion

Levelled worksheets in the Unit Assessment
Opportunities for peer- and self-review

## Keywords

> Precision
> Program
> Programmed
> Real-life situations
> Subroutine

# Resources required

 **Whole Class Presentation: Unit 5.2**

 **Written Task: Problems in control systems**
**Written Task: Problems in control systems (Suggested answers)**
**End of Unit Activity 5.2: Photobooth (L4–5)**
**End of Unit Activity 5.2: Photobooth (L5–6)**
**End of Unit Activity 5.2: Photobooth (Suggested solution)**

 **Interactive Test: Control systems in real life**

**Pages 86–9 of the Pupil's Book**

# Teaching notes

1 Use the Module 5 Case Study to introduce the module.
2 Use the Whole Class Presentation to explain the objectives of this unit and provide an overview.
3 Explain the levels of detail that pupils can go to when writing control instructions. Show the main steps involved in the pedestrian crossing on page 86 of the Pupil's Book.
4 Pupils complete the Interactive Test.
5 Use the pedestrian crossing flowchart on page 87 of the Pupil's Book to demonstrate an example of a more precise flowchart.
6 Discuss how control systems operate in real-life situations, how unexpected things can happen and that the system needs to take account of this.
7 Pupils complete the Written Task 'Problems in control systems'.
8 Pupils complete the End of Unit Activity 'Photobooth'.

# Assessment guidance for End of Unit Activity

**L4** Pupils plan and test sequences of instructions.
   They create a basic flowchart containing the main processes, although it may lack precision and efficiency. However, it should work.

**L5** Pupils create sequences of instructions and understand the need to be precise when framing and sequencing instructions.
   They create a system that works and is quite precise in that the processes are broken down into fairly detailed steps. However, it may lack efficiency. For example, instructions are repeated where perhaps a loop or subroutine could be used.

**L6** Pupils develop, try out and refine sequences of instructions and show efficiency in framing these instructions, using subroutines where appropriate.
   At L6, you are looking for an efficient and complete solution. The 'suggested answer' shows a typical L6 solution that includes the use of a subroutine. You would also expect the pupil to annotate the flowchart to show a full understanding of what is happening at each stage.

# 5.3 | Teacher's Notes
## Making control instructions more efficient

## Lesson objectives

The focus for this unit is the creation of efficient flowcharts. To achieve L6 or above, pupils must demonstrate efficiency in their instructions: the flowcharts must work fully and use as few instructions as possible.

Pupils were introduced to loops, counters and subroutines in InteraCT 1 and they may also have included them in the InteraCT 2 work they have done so far. The purpose of this unit is to consolidate this learning and to show specific examples where efficiency can be achieved.

The main way that pupils can check for efficiency is to make sure that they are not repeating instructions. If they are, it is likely that a loop should be used. A simple loop can be achieved by drawing a line back to a previous flowchart symbol. A more complex loop might be achieved using a counter, to make something happen a certain number of times.

Finally, pupils are asked to consider the use of subroutines, where they can store sets of instructions which they could use over and over again.

## PoS reference

2.2e) use ICT to make things happen by planning, testing and modifying a sequence of instructions, recognising where a group of instructions needs repeating, and automating frequently used processes by constructing efficient procedures that are fit for purpose.
2.3c) use technical terms appropriately and correctly.
2.4b) reflect on their own and others' uses of ICT to help them develop and improve their ideas and the quality of their work.
2.4c) reflect on what they have learnt and use these insights to improve future work.

## Framework reference

Developing ideas and making things happen:

> Analysing and automating processes: automate simple processes; represent simple design specifications as diagrams
> Control and monitoring: develop and test a system to monitor and control events

## STU reference

8.1, 8.6

## A&A CD-ROM reference

Strand C Activities 1–3

## PLTS

Independent enquirer
Reflective learner

## Every Child Matters

Enjoy and achieve

## Differentiation and inclusion

Levelled worksheets in the Unit Assessment
Opportunities for peer- and self-review

## Keywords

> Counter
> Efficient instructions
> Inefficient instructions
> Loop

## Resources required

 **Whole Class Presentation: Unit 5.3**

 **Written Task: Writing efficient instructions**
**Written Task: Writing efficient instructions (Suggested answers)**
**End of Unit Activity 5.3: Efficient flowcharts (L4–5)**
**End of Unit Activity 5.3: Efficient flowcharts (L5–6)**
**End of Unit Activity 5.3: Efficient flowcharts (L4–5 Suggested solution)**
**End of Unit Activity 5.3: Efficient flowcharts (L5–6 Suggested solution)**

 **Interactive Test: Loops, counters and subroutines**

**Pages 90–1 of the Pupil's Book**

## Teaching notes

1 Use the Module 5 Case Study to introduce the module.
2 Use the Whole Class Presentation to explain the objectives of this unit and provide an overview.
3 Explain the concept of efficiency in terms of writing as few instructions as possible to make the system work. Start with the green man flashing example (page 90 of the Pupil's Book). Explain how the counter is used.
4 Pupils complete the 'Writing efficient instructions' worksheet (Written Task).
5 Work through the burglar alarm example (page 91 of the Pupil's Book).
6 Pupils complete the Interactive Test.
7 Pupils complete the End of Unit Activity 'Efficient flowcharts'.

## Assessment guidance for End of Unit Activity

**L4** Pupils plan and test sequences of instructions.
  They create a basic flowchart containing the main processes, although it may lack precision and efficiency. However, it should work. A suggested L4/5 answer is provided.

**L5** Pupils create sequences of instructions and understand the need to be precise when framing and sequencing instructions.
  They create a system that works and is quite precise in that the processes are broken down into fairly detailed steps. However, it may lack efficiency. For example, instructions may be repeated where perhaps a loop or subroutine could be used.

**L6** Pupils develop, try out and refine sequences of instructions and show efficiency in framing these instructions, using subroutines where appropriate.
  At L6, you are looking for an efficient and complete solution. The 'suggested answer' shows a typical L6 solution that includes the use of a subroutine. You would also expect the pupil to annotate the flowchart to show a full understanding of what is happening at each stage.

# 5.4 Teacher's Notes
## Monitoring and control systems

## Lesson objectives

This final unit on control looks at the widespread use of control systems in everything from electronic devices through to nuclear power stations. The emphasis is not so much on how the systems work, but on the uses and the implications of using computer control.

The concept of monitoring is also introduced. This may simply be monitoring of data using sensors. It is also about the monitoring of individuals, for example, through the use of CCTV systems.

Pupils consider the advantages and disadvantages of the reliance on computer control. They also consider why some people object to the use of computers to monitor individuals.

## PoS reference

3d) develop an understanding of the need to: employ safe working practices in order to minimise physical stress; keep information secure; manage information organisation, storage and access to secure content and enable efficient retrieval.
3e) consider the impact of ICT on individuals, communities and society, including the social, economic, legal and ethical implications of access to, and use of, ICT.

## Framework reference

Developing ideas and making things happen:

> Analysing and automating processes: consider the benefits and drawbacks of using ICT to automate processes
> Control and monitoring: understand how control and monitoring has affected commercial and industrial processes

## Resources required

 **Whole Class Presentation: Unit 5.4**

 **Written Task: Monitoring and control systems**
**Written Task: Monitoring and control systems (Suggested answers)**
**End of Unit Activity 5.4: Is Big Brother watching you?**

 **Interactive Test: Control and monitoring systems**

**Pages 92–5 of the Pupil's Book**

## STU reference

8.1, 8.6

## A&A CD-ROM reference

Strand C Activities 1–3

## PLTS

Independent enquirer
Reflective learner

## Every Child Matters

Enjoy and achieve

## Differentiation and inclusion

Levelled worksheets in the Unit Assessment

## Keywords

> Big Brother
> Control system
> Monitoring
> Monitoring and control system
> System failure

# Teaching notes

1 Use the Module 5 Case Study to introduce the module.
2 Use the Whole Class Presentation to explain the objectives of this unit and provide an overview.
3 Recap on the widespread use of computer control in everything from calculators to aeroplanes.
4 Explain what monitoring is and how it links with control.
5 Pupils complete the Written Task 'Monitoring and control systems'.
6 Discuss the advantages and disadvantages of using computer control. Pupils should be able to contribute ideas. Discuss the Big Brother concept and ask pupils for their opinions.
7 Pupils complete the Interactive Test.
8 Pupils complete the End of Unit Activity 'Is Big Brother watching you?'.
9 Pupils complete the End of Module Assignment.

# Assessment guidance for End of Unit Activity

This activity is more related to the wider implications of the use of computer control and monitoring. It allows pupils to demonstrate capability at L4 and 5. Module 6 deals in more detail with these issues and allows pupils to demonstrate capability up to L6.

**L4** Pupils understand the risks associated with communicating digitally, including the security of personal information.

They may indicate that they can be monitored by CCTV and other methods. They may have difficulty explaining why this may be an issue.

**L5** Pupils use ICT safely and responsibly. They discuss their knowledge and experience of using ICT and their observations of its use outside school.

Pupils show a greater awareness of a wide range of issues in relation to monitoring. They demonstrate some empathy with the wider issues rather than talking in personal terms about being monitored and recorded.

# 6 | Teacher's Notes
## Wider aspects of ICT

## Module structure

This module is wide-ranging and covers various aspects of ICT and how it is used in the wider world. It covers those aspects referenced in the 'Range and Content' section of the Programme of Study.

6.1 Misuse of personal data
6.2 Health and safety issues
6.3 Plagiarism and copyright
6.4 Social impact of ICT

Unit 6.1 looks at the topical issue of misuse of personal data, covering everything from unsolicited mail through to identity theft. Unit 6.2 considers health and safety issues in relation to the use of ICT. Unit 6.3 considers plagiarism and copyright, with particular reference to information collected from the Internet. Finally, Unit 6.4 looks at issues relating to equal access to ICT and what effect it has on employment here and in other countries.

As with all the modules, there are some module resources that you can use before you start on the units. These are:

> Module 6 Case Study
> Module 6 Starter Activities

## Assessment

All assessments in this module are designed to allow pupils to demonstrate levels 4 to 6. There are levelled Unit Assessments and interpretation of the levels is provided in the Teacher's Notes for each unit.

There is also a levelled Module Assignment that pupils can work on when all the units are complete. This is designed to cover all aspects of this module. This is a differentiated activity and you should give each pupil the worksheet that is most appropriate to the level that you think they are working towards. The interpretation of levels for the Module Assignment is given below.

## Assessment guidance for Module Assignment

**L4** Pupils understand the risks associated with communicating digitally, including the security of personal information.

At this level pupils may find it difficult to comment on anything other than their own direct experience. They should complete the diary but may find the questions difficult.

**L5** Pupils discuss their knowledge and experience of using ICT and their observations of its use outside school.

At this level pupils should show an understanding of the use of ICT in and out of school. They should complete the diary and be able to answer the first two questions.

**L6** Pupils discuss the impact of ICT on society.

Pupils should be able to complete the worksheet unaided.

# Suggested answers to questions posed in the Case Study

How do you think each member of the family might use ICT? Why might there be differences in what they each use ICT for?

**Suggested answers:**

The children may use ICT for their school and college work including: using the Internet for research; using word processing to type up homework and essays.

The children may use the computer for entertainment purposes: music, video, chatting.

The parents may use the computers in their jobs. In particular, the dad may use databases and spreadsheets as part of his work.

The parents may use ICT to keep in touch with family and friends using email.

The grandparents may be less likely to use ICT as they are older. However, the older generation is also using ICT – the Internet and email in particular.

Why might Maalik get lots of junk mail? Where did the credit card companies get his name and address from? Why do you think the bank is asking Maalik to repay money that he has not even spent?

**Suggested answers:**

He might get junk mail because businesses might think that he might buy their products. The credit card companies probably got his name from other credit card companies or banks. They could get it out of the phone book or from other databases that he is listed on.

Maalik may be the victim of fraud or identify theft. It looks like someone has borrowed money using his name and personal details. They may have got them from him when he was online.

What health and safety problems might there be with what Jamie is doing? What would you do to make the computer area a bit safer and more comfortable?

**Suggested answers:**

Jamie may be spending too much of his time on the computer, which could lead to eye strain, headaches or other strain injuries. He may get unfit and overweight if he does not do enough exercise. It might also be a bit anti-social if he spends too much time on the computer.

There are some health hazards with the way he is working. The sockets have too many plugs and he has fluids near electricity. If he spilt something on the computer, he could get an electric shock. The

computer area is very cluttered so this could happen. There are also lots of wires trailing around which he could trip over.

He should keep all fluids away from the computers, tidy up the space on the computer desk, tidy the cables up and have fewer things plugged into the sockets.

Why might what Jamie has just done be wrong? Why might it be illegal? How could Jamie make sure that he does not do anything wrong or illegal when getting information, images and music from the Internet?

**Suggested answers:**

He cannot just copy and paste whole blocks of text without putting it into his own words. The text and the images he has used may belong to someone else and he should check the copyright.

The music downloads may be illegal if he is not getting them from a legal site. This usually means that he would have to pay for the download.

Why might some people in the UK not have access to ICT? Why might some people in other countries not have access to ICT? What could be done to help these people get access to ICT?

**Suggested answers:**

> They may be poor and unable to afford a computer.
> They may not have the necessary skills and education to use ICT.
> They may live in a developing country where they don't have electricity, computers or phone lines for the Internet.
> They may be elderly and have never had any training in ICT.
> They may have disabilities, e.g. impaired vision which mean that standard ICT equipment is not adequate.
> They may have religious objections to the use of ICT.

To help them:

> Government schemes can provide training and funding.
> Computers and the Internet can be made available through schools and libraries.
> Training courses can be provided for anyone that wants them.
> Charitable funding can be sent to developing countries so they can afford the equipment.

# 6.1 | Teacher's Notes
## Misuse of personal data

## Lesson objectives

This unit looks at the issue of personal data, how they can be misused and how to protect them. The unit starts with a definition of what personal data are. Some examples are given and pupils should be encouraged to think about other data that are personal or sensitive. The unit explains why the data needs to be collected, but also how they can be misused.

The unit then considers the different ways that data can be misused – anything from data being sold for marketing purposes through to full-scale identity theft and fraud. Pupils complete a written task specifically on the dangers of identity theft.

The unit then looks at the main principles of the Data Protection Act before looking at ways in which they can protect their own personal data.

## PoS reference

2.2a) select and use ICT tools and techniques appropriately, safely and efficiently.

3d) develop an understanding of the need to: employ safe working practices in order to minimise physical stress; keep information secure; manage information organisation, storage and access to secure content and enable efficient retrieval.

3e) consider the impact of ICT on individuals, communities and society, including the social, economic, legal and ethical implications of access to, and use of, ICT.

## Framework reference

Finding things out:

> Organising and investigating: understand how data collection and storage are automated; understand the impact of electronic databases on commercial practice and society; understand the potential misuse of personal data

## STU reference

None

## A&A CD-ROM reference

None

## PLTS

Independent enquirer
Reflective learner
Creative thinker

## Every Child Matters

Enjoy and achieve
Achieve economic well being

## Differentiation and inclusion

Opportunities for peer- and self-review

## Keywords

> Anti-phishing software
> Data misuse
> Data Protection Act
> Data Protection Registrar
> Firewall
> Identity (ID) theft
> Password
> Personal data and information
> Phishing
> Sensitive data and information
> Spyware

# Resources required

**Whole Class Presentation: Unit 6.1**

**Written Task: Misuse of data**
**Written Task: Misuse of data (Suggested answers)**
**End of Unit Activity 6.1: Keeping personal data safe**
**End of Unit Activity 6.1: Keeping personal data safe (Suggested answers)**

**Interactive Test: The Data Protection Act**

**Pages 100–101 of the Pupil's Book**

# Teaching notes

1 Use the Module 6 Case Study to introduce pupils to the issues.
2 Use the Whole Class Presentation to explain the objectives of this unit and provide an overview.
3 Explain what personal data are and ask pupils for examples. Explain why personal data are collected, e.g. by the school or a doctor, but also how these data could then be misused.
4 Pupils complete the Written Task 'Misuse of data'.
5 Explain the Data Protection Act and its main principles.
6 Pupils complete the Interactive Test.
7 Discuss what pupils can do themselves to protect their personal data.
8 Pupils complete the End of Unit Activity 'Keeping personal data safe'.

# Assessment guidance for End of Unit Activity

This activity allows pupils to demonstrate capability at L4 and 5.

**L4** Pupils understand the risks associated with communicating digitally, including the security of personal information.
  They may be able to partly complete the table, perhaps only thinking of one or two issues, or perhaps completing the first column but not the second.

**L5** Pupils use ICT safely and responsibly. They discuss their knowledge and experience of using ICT and their observations of its use outside school.
  They should be able to identify at least four issues and complete both columns.

# 6.2 | Teacher's Notes
## Health and safety issues

## Lesson objectives

This unit focuses on health and safety issues in relation to computer use. Pupils are introduced to the concept of health and safety and how incorrect use or over-use of computers can lead to physical or mental issues.

The unit divides the problems into three categories: physical injury (through accidents caused by electricity or trailing cables); physical strains (through over-use or incorrect positioning of the computer and the user) and stress (through having too much work to do in too short a time).

The problems are listed and solutions to each problem are explained.

## PoS reference

3d) develop an understanding of the need to: employ safe working practices in order to minimise physical stress; keep information secure; manage information organisation, storage and access to secure content and enable efficient retrieval.

3e) consider the impact of ICT on individuals, communities and society, including the social, economic, legal and ethical implications of access to, and use of, ICT.

## Framework reference

None

## STU reference

None

## A&A CD-ROM reference

None

## PLTS

Independent enquirer
Reflective learner
Creative thinker

## Every Child Matters

Be healthy
Stay safe
Enjoy and achieve
Achieve economic well-being

## Differentiation and inclusion

Opportunities for peer- and self-review

## Keywords

> Health and Safety
> Health and Safety Policy
> Physical injury
> Physical strain
> RSI (Repetitive strain injury)
> Stress

# Resources required

**Whole Class Presentation: Unit 6.2**

**Written Task: Health and safety policy**
**Written Task: Health and safety policy (Suggested answers)**
**End of Unit Activity 6.2: Health and safety and you**

**Interactive Test: Health and safety issues**

**Pages 102–105 of the Pupil's Book**

# Teaching notes

1 Use the Module 6 Case Study to introduce pupils to the issues.
2 Use the Whole Class Presentation to explain the objectives of this unit and provide an overview.
3 Explain the concept of health and safety and how it applies to computer use. Explain how there are different levels of risk (serious injury, strain injury and stress). Discuss the risks and what pupils can do about them.
4 Pupils complete the Interactive Test.
5 Pupils complete the Written Task 'Health and safety policy'.
6 Pupils complete the End of Unit Activity 'Health and safety and you'.

# Assessment guidance for End of Unit Activity

The level descriptions only cover health and safety issues at L5. If pupils provide sensible answers, they can be awarded L5 in this aspect of the programme of study.

**L5** Pupils use ICT safely and responsibly. They discuss their knowledge and experience of using ICT and their observations of its use outside school. Pupils provide sensible answers to most of the questions.

# 6.3 | Teacher's Notes
## Plagiarism and copyright

## Lesson objectives

This unit focuses on plagiarism and copyright. The two concepts are very closely related. The concept of 'plagiarism' is explained as copying someone else's work and then pretending that you did it. Pupils should be quite familiar with this through the use of websites and the copy and paste technique for completing homework assignments. Pupils work through why plagiarism is wrong and what they can do to avoid being accused of it.

The unit then looks at copyright and how this applies to any creative work including books, music and film. Pupils are asked to consider their own use of material and to consider why copyright law exists, and how they can make sure that they do not break the law.

## PoS reference

2.1a) consider systematically the information needed to solve a problem, complete a task or answer a question, and explore how it will be used.
2.1b) use and refine search methods to obtain information that is well matched to purpose, by selecting appropriate sources.
2.1c) collect and enter quantitative and qualitative information, checking its accuracy.
2.1d) analyse and evaluate information, judging its value, accuracy, plausibility and bias.
2.3b) communicate and exchange information (including digital communication) effectively, safely and responsibly.
2.4c) reflect on what they have learnt and use these insights to improve future work.
3b) use a variety of information sources, including large data sets, in a range of contexts.
3e) consider the impact of ICT on individuals, communities and society, including the social, economic, legal and ethical implications of access to, and use of, ICT.

## Framework reference

Finding things out:

> Using data and information sources: understand how the content and style of an information source affect its suitability for particular purposes

## STU reference

None

## A&A CD-ROM reference

None

## PLTS

Reflective learner

## Every Child Matters

Stay safe

## Differentiation and inclusion

Opportunities for peer- and self-review

## Keywords

> Copyright
> Downloading
> Plagiarism
> Research

# Resources required

 **Whole Class Presentation: Unit 6.3**

 **Written Task: Plagiarism**
**Written Task: Plagiarism (Suggested answers)**
**End of Unit Activity 6.3: Copyright and you**
**End of Unit Activity 6.3: Copyright and you (Suggested answers)**

 **Interactive Test: Copyright**

**Pages 106–107 of the Pupil's Book**

# Teaching notes

1 Use the Module 6 Case Study to introduce pupils to the issues.
2 Use the Whole Class Presentation to explain the objectives of this unit and provide an overview.
3 Explain the concept of plagiarism.
4 Pupils complete the Written Task 'Plagiarism'.
5 Explain the concept of copyright.
6 Pupils complete the Interactive Test.
7 Pupils complete the End of Unit Activity 'Copyright and you'.

# Assessment guidance for End of Unit Activity

**L4** Pupils understand the risks associated with communicating digitally, including the security of personal information. They plan and test sequences of instructions.

They should show an awareness of the issues of plagiarism and copyright. Typically, they should be able to answer questions 1 and 2 effectively.

**L5** Pupils use ICT safely and responsibly. They discuss their knowledge and experience of using ICT and their observations of its use outside school.

They should show some empathy with other people as well as understanding the implications to themselves. They should be able to answer all the questions effectively.

# 6.4

## Teacher's Notes
## Social impact of ICT

### Lesson objectives

This units focuses on the impact of ICT on employment. It looks at the jobs that ICT has created and the jobs that have been lost as a direct result of ICT use. Pupils look at some of the winners and losers in the workplace. This covers all aspects of ICT including the increased use of ICT for shopping and banking and the use of ICT in factories.

This unit also looks at the impact of ICT across the world, looking in particular at the experience of developing countries compared to developed countries. India is used as an example of a country that has now developed ICT to become world leaders. The impact that this has on UK workers is examined.

### PoS reference

3e) consider the impact of ICT on individuals, communities and society, including the social, economic, legal and ethical implications of access to, and use of, ICT.

### Framework reference

Finding things out:

> Organising and investigating: understand how data collection and storage are automated; understand the impact of electronic databases on commercial practice and society; understand the potential misuse of personal data

### STU reference

None

### A&A CD-ROM reference

None

### PLTS

Independent enquirer
Reflective learner

### Every Child Matters

None

### Differentiation and inclusion

Opportunities for peer- and self-review

### Keywords

> Computer technician
> Developed countries
> Developing countries
> Digital divide
> Employment
> ICT access
> Newly industrialised countries
> Redundant
> Workplace

## Resources required

**Whole Class Presentation: Unit 6.4**

**Written Task: ICT in developing countries**
**Written Task: ICT in developing countries (Suggested answers)**
**End of Unit Activity 6.4: The impact of ICT**
**End of Unit Activity 6.4: The impact of ICT (Suggested answers)**

**Interactive Test: The wider impact of ICT**

**Pages 108–109 of the Pupil's Book**

## Teaching notes

1 Use the Module 6 Case Study to introduce pupils to the issues.

3 Use the Whole Class Presentation to explain the objectives of this unit and provide an overview.

3 Explain the concept of employment and how ICT affects it. It is important to view ICT in its widest context here rather than simply looking at the use of PCs and the Internet. Work through the winners and losers and ask pupils for their own examples.

4 Pupils complete the Interactive Test.

5 Explain the concept of access to ICT and discuss with pupils why some people in this country might not have access. Widen this to a discussion about the use of ICT around the world. Some discussion of developed and developing countries is needed here.

6 Pupils complete the Written Task 'ICT in developing countries'.

7 Pupils complete the End of Unit Activity 'Impact of ICT'.

8 Pupils complete the End of Module Assignment.

## Assessment guidance for End of Unit Activity

**L4** Pupils compare their use of ICT with other methods and with its use outside school.
   They may find it difficult to offer answers to questions that are outside their direct experience. Consequently, they may struggle to answer questions 2 to 5.

**L5** Pupils discuss their knowledge and experience of using ICT and their observations of its use outside school.
   They should show an awareness of issues outside their own direct experience.

**L6** Pupils discuss the impact of ICT on society.
   At this level you would expect sensible answers to all five questions.

# 7 Teacher's Notes
## Integrated Tasks

## Module structure

The format of the Integrated Tasks is slightly different from the other modules. These tasks provide an opportunity for pupils to demonstrate their ICT capability across a range of ICT topics. These tasks take a scenario as a main theme and then break this down into assignments that pupils will work on over several lessons. Pupils can complete all the assignments, or you can pick and choose which parts you would like them to complete.

The chosen scenarios are quite open-ended in terms of the ways that ICT could be used. A suitable starter activity would be to watch the introductions and ask pupils to identify ways in which ICT could be used in the given scenario.

There are two or three assignments in each Integrated Task and these provide pupils with opportunities to demonstrate ICT capability from Levels 3–6. Assessment Guidance is provided for each assignment within each Integrated Task.

The assignments are presented to the pupils using worksheets. Note that there are three versions of every worksheet depending on the level that you think pupils are working towards. The three versions are L3/4, L4/5 and L5/6.

They have been split like this for two reasons. First, it means that each activity will provide opportunities for pupils to work towards the level above their current one. For example, the L3 pupil will work on a L3/4 task, which means that as the task progresses, they will work towards L4. The second reason is that it is sometimes difficult to assess pupil levels in each strand of ICT before a pupil starts, so by splitting them in this way, it means that a pupil is more likely to be given an activity that is commensurate with their ability.

The Integrated Tasks give pupils the chance to work autonomously and devise their own solutions to the problems they are presented with. They should be encouraged to use the skills and knowledge that they have gained during the course.

The three integrated tasks are:

> The catalogue shop – this covers data handling, presentation and control.
> Choose and Book – this covers data handling and web design.
> Weather forecasting – this covers web research and modelling.

## Building up a portfolio

Pupils should be encouraged to use sensible file naming conventions and to store files in suitable folder structures. Effectively they are creating an e-portfolio of evidence as they work through these integrated tasks. Pupils should also be creating separate backups of their work as it progresses.

# Teaching notes

The following notes are applicable to all three units of the Intregrated Tasks.

1 Use the Whole Class Presentation to explain the objectives of these integrated tasks and provide an overview.
2 The narrative lists the main processes involved with the scenario. It is advised that the three assignments are tackled in order.
3 Pupils can work at their own pace, so more able pupils may complete all three assignments whereas less able pupils may complete one or two of them.
4 You need to allocate around one hour for each assignment although, as the assignments are quite open-ended, this time could be extended.

## Resources required: Unit 7.1

**Whole Class Presentation: Unit 7.1**

**Task 1: Designing a page of the catalogue (L3–4)**
**Task 1: Designing a page of the catalogue (L4–5)**
**Task 1: Designing a page of the catalogue (L5–6)**
**Task 1: New paddling pool information**
**Task 1: Paddling pools**

**Task 2: Controlling the self-service kiosk (L3–4)**
**Task 2: Controlling the self-service kiosk (L4–5)**
**Task 2: Controlling the self-service kiosk (L5–6)**
**Task 3: Screen designs (L3–4)**
**Task 3: Screen designs (L4–5)**
**Task 3: Screen designs (L5–6)**

**Pages 112–13 of the Pupil's Book**

## Resources required: Unit 7.2

**Whole Class Presentation: Unit 7.2**

**Task 1: GP database (L3-4)**
**Task 1: GP database (L4-5)**
**Task 1: GP database (L5-6)**
**Task 1: X-ray booking database (Excel)**
**Task 1: X-ray booking database (Access)**

**Task 1: GP database (L3-4 Answer)**
**Task 1: GP database (L4-5 Answer)**
**Task 1: GP database (L5-6 Answer)**
**Task 2: Choose and Book website (L3-4)**
**Task 2: Choose and Book website (L4-5)**
**Task 2: Choose and Book website (L5-6)**

**Pages 114–5 of the Pupil's Book**

## Resources required: Unit 7.3

**Whole Class Presentation: Unit 7.3**

**Task 1: Hurricane research (L3–4)**
**Task 1: Hurricane research (L4–5)**
**Task 1: Hurricane research (L5–6)**
**Task 2: Hurricane model (L3–4)**
**Task 2: Hurricane model (L4–5)**
**Task 2: Hurricane model (L5–6)**

**Task 2: Hurricane model (L3–4 Answers)**
**Task 2: Hurricane model (L4–5 Answers)**
**Task 2: Hurricane model (L5–6 Answers)**
**Task 2: The Hurricane predictor spreadsheet**
**Task 2: The Hurricane predictor spreadsheet (L5–6 Solution)**

**Pages 116–17 of the Pupil's Book**

# 7.1 Teacher's Notes
## The catalogue shop

## Lesson objectives

This is the first of three Integrated Tasks. The format of these is different from the Modules, as students work autonomously, solving a range of problems in a given scenario.

The scenario for this task is a catalogue shop. It might help students to think of Argos as an example. The main uses of ICT within this scenario and for the three assignments are:

Task 1: Designing a page of the catalogue – this covers finding and presenting information.
Task 2: Controlling the self-service kiosk – this covers control.
Task 3: Screen designs – this covers presenting information.

Pupils should tackle these tasks in order, producing a portfolio of evidence as they work through. Pupils can work individually or in pairs on these assignments, asking for your help when needed.

## PoS reference

**Task 1 Designing a page of the catalogue**
2.1a) consider systematically the information needed to solve a problem, complete a task or answer a question, and explore how it will be used.
2.1b) use and refine search methods to obtain information that is well matched to purpose, by selecting appropriate sources.
2.1c) collect and enter quantitative and qualitative information, checking its accuracy.
2.1d) analyse and evaluate information, judging its value, accuracy, plausibility and bias.
2.2a) select and use ICT tools and techniques appropriately, safely and efficiently.
2.2b) solve problems by developing, exploring and structuring information, and deriving new information for a particular purpose.
2.2f) bring together, draft and refine information, including through the combination of text, sound and image.
2.3a) use a range of ICT tools to present information in forms that are fit for purpose, meet audience needs and suit the content.
2.4b) reflect on their own and others' uses of ICT to help them develop and improve their ideas and the quality of their work.
3c) use and review of the effectiveness of different ICT tools, including a range of software applications, in terms of meeting user needs and solving problems.

**Task 2 Controlling the self-service kiosk**
2.2e) use ICT to make things happen by planning, testing and modifying a sequence of instructions, recognising where a group of instructions needs repeating, and automating frequently used processes by constructing efficient procedures that are fit for purpose.
2.3c) use technical terms appropriately and correctly.

## A&A CD-ROM reference
I

## PLTS
Independent enquirer
Creative thinker
Reflective learner
Team worker (if working collaboratively)
Self-manager
Effective participator

## Every Child Matters
Enjoy and achieve
Achieve economic well-being

## Differentiation and inclusion
Opportunities for peer- and self-review

## Keywords
> Keypad
> Self-service kiosk
> Stock database
> User interface
> Visual display

**Task 3 Screen designs**

2.2a) select and use ICT tools and techniques appropriately, safely and efficiently.

2.2d) design information systems and suggest improvements to existing systems.

2.3a) use a range of ICT tools to present information in forms that are fit for purpose, meet audience needs and suit the content.

2.3b) communicate and exchange information (including digital communication) effectively, safely and responsibly.

2.3c) use technical terms appropriately and correctly.

2.4c) reflect on what they have learnt and use these insights to improve future work.

3c) use and review of the effectiveness of different ICT tools, including a range of software applications, in terms of meeting user needs and solving problems.

## Assessment guidance for Task 1

**L3** Pupils should be able to find and use appropriate stored information. This means they should be able to identify the correct photograph and text needed and copy and paste this into the appropriate part of the leaflet. They should re-size the image and add text as appropriate.

They should be able to save the file into a folder using a suitable file name. They may create this folder or place it in an existing one. Guidance could be needed to explain folder structures.

**L4** Pupils should need little guidance in creating the new page. The amount of guidance you have to give determines if they are working at L4. Pupils may make fairly fundamental changes to the layout, changes in font style, colours and sizes, the introduction of more colour, a greater use of photographs and graphics. There could also be changes in the style of language that is used.

**L5** Pupils should be able to select the most appropriate software although some discussion may take place about whether to use a word processor or a desktop-publishing package.

They should be able to find the information they need from the information sheet and perhaps from websites and copy and paste it into an appropriate place on the leaflet. The information should be correct. They should be selective in the information they copy across. The amount of information given should be appropriate for this kind of publication so they should select the information that is relevant and synthesise it.

**L6** Pupils create a suitable page with little or no help from the teacher. They select the most appropriate software and information, using a range of sources.

They must show a very clear sense of audience and their design must be appropriate. They should be able to explain the choices they have made and how the design of the page is suitable for the stated purpose and audience.

Pupils should demonstrate the use of efficiency tools where possible.

## Assessment guidance for Task 2

**L3** Pupils should be able to create a simple set of instructions or a flowchart to show most of the basic processes involved. They may need to write this as a series of steps before turning it into a flowchart.

They may need guidance in selecting the appropriate flowcharting symbols in the first instance but should create a system that shows the main steps involved in the purchasing process.

**L4** Pupils should be able to incorporate all of the processes needed to create the system although it may lack efficiency. For example, setting off a siren and then switching on lights would be done more efficiently through a sub-process or macro, but at L4, they are unlikely to have done this. However, the flowchart should show a system that would work effectively. This may include the use of a loop.

**L5** Pupils should be more autonomous in the design of the system, being able to select the appropriate input and output devices and putting them together into an efficient system. They should be able to translate the requirements into an appropriate system.

You would expect 'precision' in the L5 response with the pupil creating a system that would work in every aspect. They should add comments to their flowcharts that demonstrate an understanding of every process and a justification of what devices they have chosen.

**L6** Pupils should be able to design and then implement a system from scratch, selecting the most appropriate devices for the task. They should show efficiency in their instructions. You would expect them to be using subroutines for repeated instructions within the flowchart.

A feature of a pupil working at L6 is that they independently refine the instructions until they have created the most efficient solution. They should add comments to their flowcharts that demonstrate an understanding of every process.

## Assessment guidance for Task 3

**L3** Pupils should be able to make the user interface from scratch although they may need some guidance in ensuring that all relevant features have been included. They may need some guidance in selecting which software to use in order to create the interface.

**L4** Pupils should need little guidance in creating a user interface, creating a suitable mix of graphics and text for the purpose. Their finished user interface shows some consideration for the chosen user.

**L5** Pupils should be able to translate the specification in the worksheet into a design for a user interface. They should be able to create two out of the three user interfaces from the list provided on the worksheet.

They make decisions about the information needed for each one, select an appropriate style of language, and use images and sounds appropriately for the purpose.

Pupils should be able to evaluate their work, explaining what they have done to ensure their interfaces are suitable for purpose and audience. This may include use of fonts, styles and sizes, use of colour, use of photographs and other images, the language style used, and the amount of information provided.

**L6** Pupils create a separate user interface which is clearly designed for the purpose in each case. They must show a very clear sense of audience.

An important factor at L6 is that the pupil explains what decisions they have made and why.

**Typical solutions**

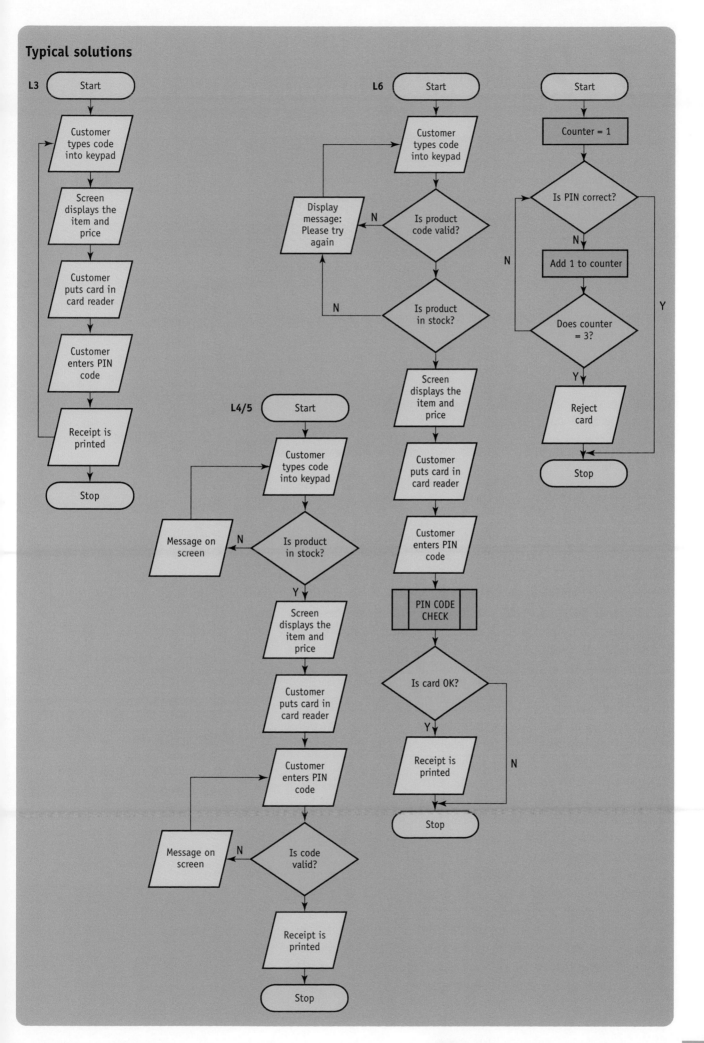

# 7.2 Teacher's Notes
## Choose and Book

## Lesson objectives

This is the second of three Integrated Tasks. The format of these is different from the Modules, as students work autonomously, solving a range of problems in a given scenario.

The scenario for this task is a medical appointments booking system. This system is fictitious but is based on the 'Choose and Book' system operated by the NHS. The main uses of ICT within this scenario and for the two assignments are:

Task 1: GP database – this covers setting up a database and using it to find information and test hypotheses.
Task 2: Choose and Book website – this covers the design and creation of web pages.

Pupils should tackle these tasks in order, producing a portfolio of evidence as they work through. Pupils can work individually or in pairs on these assignments, asking for your help when needed.

## PoS reference

### Task 1 GP database

2.1a) consider systematically the information needed to solve a problem, complete a task or answer a question, and explore how it will be used.
2.1b) use and refine search methods to obtain information that is well matched to purpose, by selecting appropriate sources.
2.1c) collect and enter quantitative and qualitative information, checking its accuracy.
2.1d) analyse and evaluate information, judging its value, accuracy, plausibility and bias.
2.2b) solve problems by developing, exploring and structuring information, and deriving new information for a particular purpose.
2.2d) design information systems and suggest improvements to existing systems.
3a) use a range of information, with different characteristics, structures and purposes, and evaluation of how it matches requirements and its fitness for purpose.
3b) use a variety of information sources, including large data sets, in a range of contexts.
3c) use and review of the effectiveness of different ICT tools, including a range of software applications, in terms of meeting user needs and solving problems.
3d) develop an understanding of the need to: employ safe working practices in order to minimise physical stress; keep information secure; manage information organisation, storage and access to secure content and enable efficient retrieval.

## A&A CD-ROM reference

I

## PLTS

Independent enquirer
Creative thinker
Reflective learner
Team worker (if working collaboratively)
Self-manager
Effective participator

## Every Child Matters

Enjoy and achieve
Achieve economic well-being

## Differentiation and inclusion

Opportunities for peer- and self-review

## Keywords

None

**Task 2 Choose and Book website**

2.1a) consider systematically the information needed to solve a problem, complete a task or answer a question, and explore how it will be used.

2.2a) select and use ICT tools and techniques appropriately, safely and efficiently.

2.2f) bring together, draft and refine information, including through the combination of text, sound and image.

2.3b) communicate and exchange information (including digital communication) effectively, safely and responsibly.

2.4c) reflect on what they have learnt and use these insights to improve future work.

## Assessment guidance for Task 1

**L3** Pupils may need considerable help in working out what fields are required and what data types to use. They should be able to carry out a sort using a single criterion and a query using one criterion although some guidance may be needed. They should be able to read off the resulting answer to answer the questions.

**L4** Pupils should be able to identify the main fields that are needed. They should be able to choose the most appropriate data types for most questions with little or no guidance. They should be able to carry out simple sorts and queries largely unaided, perhaps requiring some guidance in the early stages. They should be able to carry out slightly more sophisticated queries using 'greater than' or 'less than'. They should be able to carry out a more complex query using two criteria and a single AND or OR operator.

**L5** Pupils should be able to identify what data is needed and create the database form largely unaided, selecting suitable questions with the most appropriate data type in each case. They may need prompting to add validation checks. They should be able to carry out complex queries, combining them with sorts as required. They can work with two or three criteria and combine AND and OR operators as required.

**L6** Pupils create the database unaided selecting the most appropriate data types and adding validation checks. They should be able to carry out complex queries, combining them with sorts as required. They can work with two or three criteria and combine AND and OR operators as required. They can test hypotheses by constructing queries and comparing the results of different queries. They may create queries from existing queries, demonstrating efficiency.

## Assessment guidance for Task 2

**L3** Pupils should be able to make the web page from scratch. They should be able to find and use appropriate stored information. This means they should be able to identify appropriate text, graphics, images and sounds needed for the website. They may find it difficult to decide how much information to put on the page. Pupils should be able to save the file into a folder using a suitable file name. They may create this folder or place it in an existing one. Guidance could be needed to explain folder structures. They should be able to comment on other people's websites that they review, although this may be at a fairly superficial level. They may need considerable guidance in incorporating features into their web pages that they have seen on other sites. The finished web page may lack a consistent layout but should incorporate all the main features required.

**L4** Pupils should need little guidance in creating the new web page. They may include the appropriate font sizes and styles, or graphics that draw attention to particular sections of text. They may also write the text in a style that is appropriate to young people. They should perform meaningful reviews of other people's websites and be able to make some changes to their own website based on feedback.

**L5** Pupils are required to design and produce the website from scratch showing a clear awareness of the purpose of the pages. They should clearly explain the features that they like and don't like about other people's sites and be able to incorporate feedback from others into their own work.

**L6** The key characteristic is that pupils should work entirely independently on all aspects of this task. They should create professional-looking web pages with clear navigation between the pages. They incorporate a range of design features, which may only be limited by the capabilities of the software available. They can review other pupils' work in depth and address all feedback.

# 7.3

## Teacher's Notes
## Predicting the weather

## Lesson objectives

This is the third of three Integrated Tasks. The format of these is different from the Modules, as pupils work autonomously, solving a range of problems in a given scenario.

The scenario for this task is predicting the weather. The main uses of ICT within this scenario and for the two assignments are:

Task 1: Hurricane research – this covers finding and presenting information.

Task 2: Hurricane model – this covers using and refining a model.

Predicting the weather is a complex process that involves large-scale data collection and sophisticated modelling. The purpose of this task is for students to carry out some research into the factors that are involved with weather prediction and, in particular, with predicting hurricanes. This is an Internet research exercise leading to the students creating a presentation of some sort. In the first instance this is a multimedia slideshow, but it can be expanded to include other types of presentation.

The second part of the task is to work with and extend a model that is used to predict hurricanes. The model includes some of the factors that are used in real life and pupils work on the model to make it more realistic, based on the research they have carried out.

## PoS reference

### Task 1 Hurricane research

2.1a) consider systematically the information needed to solve a problem, complete a task or answer a question, and explore how it will be used.

2.2a) select and use ICT tools and techniques appropriately, safely and efficiently.

2.2d) design information systems and suggest improvements to existing systems.

2.2f) bring together, draft and refine information, including through the combination of text, sound and image.

2.3a) use a range of ICT tools to present information in forms that are fit for purpose, meet audience needs and suit the content.

2.3b) communicate and exchange information (including digital communication) effectively, safely and responsibly.

2.3c) use technical terms appropriately and correctly.

2.4a) review, modify and evaluate work as it progresses, reflecting critically and using feedback.

2.4b) reflect on their own and others' uses of ICT to help them develop and improve their ideas and the quality of their work.

3c) use and review of the effectiveness of different ICT tools, including a range of software applications, in terms of meeting user needs and solving problems.

## A&A CD-ROM reference

I

## PLTS

Independent enquirer
Creative thinker
Reflective learner
Team worker (if working collaboratively)
Self-manager
Effective participator

## Every Child Matters

Enjoy and achieve
Achieve economic well-being

## Differentiation and inclusion

Opportunities for peer- and self-review

## Keywords

> Forecast
> Prediction
> Supercomputer

**Task 2 Hurricane model**

2.2c) test predictions and discover patterns and relationships, exploring, evaluating and developing models by changing their rules and values.

2.4c) reflect on what they have learnt and use these insights to improve future work.

## Assessment guidance for Task 1

**L3** Pupils should be able to make the presentation from scratch showing appropriate selection of layout for each slide, font sizes and styles and use of colour. They may need some guidance initially. They should be able to find and use appropriate stored information. This means that they should be able to identify the appropriate information. They may find it difficult to synthesize the textual information but they should be able to produce some relevant bullet points. They may copy and paste all the information they can find without considering its relevance. Pupils should be able to save the file into a folder using a suitable file name. They may create this folder or place it in an existing one. Guidance could be needed to explain folder structures. Pupils may need considerable guidance in completion of the review sheet. Their responses may be fairly basic.

**L4** Pupils should need little guidance in creating a new presentation, making appropriate selection of layouts, fonts and use of colour. They should be able to select the most appropriate information for the audience. They should be able to explain some of the things they have done to appeal to the target audience. They should be able to complete a meaningful review of others' work and take into account some of the feedback on their own presentations.

**L5** Pupils should create a multimedia presentation that is clearly designed for purpose and audience. They should evaluate others' work and respond to feedback to make improvements to their own.

**L6** The key to L6 is the ability to create two very separate presentations, one for each audience. They should be very selective about the information and styles, using different information for the different audiences. They should be able to provide detailed reviews of others' work and take into account all the feedback they receive.

## Assessment guidance for Task 2

**L3** L3 modelling tasks are characterised by an ability to explore ICT-based models to find things out and solve problems. Pupils should change values within a model and read off the results. They should be able to answer Questions 1 to 4 relatively easily as they are told what settings to put in and they must then read off the answer. They need to demonstrate they understand the model, by changing values in one cell and reading off the changed values in another. Questions 5–10 require pupils to use trial and error. Pupils may need considerable help with these questions.

**L4** L4 modelling tasks are characterised by an ability to explore patterns and relationships in ICT-based models. Pupils are required to add in some new values and see what effect this has on the model. Questions 4 to 10 on the L3/4 worksheet (1 to 7 on the L4/5 worksheet) are designed primarily for L4 pupils as they are required to change values to find a solution. They should be able to change the values in the model, reading off the correct answer.

**L5** L5 modelling tasks are characterised by an ability to explore the effects of changing the variables in ICT-based models to find things out and solve problems. Questions 7–10 of the L4/5 version (1–4 of the L5/6 version) require pupils to adjust the variables and then extend the model to include a new variable. They should be able to add the new data to the lookup tables and alter the lookup formulae to take account of the changes.

**L6** Pupils should be able to make changes to the model by adding in new variables unaided. They should also consider how the model could be made more realistic either by changing the rules or by adding variables. They should be able to consider real-life factors and explain how this would make the model more realistic. They should identify that the model could be tested over time to refine and improve it.

**DL** DYNAMIC LEARNING © Hodder Education 2008

## MODULE 1 KEYWORDS

| | |
|:---:|:---:|
| Fact | Validity |
| Opinion | Hits |
| Reliable | Keywords |
| URL | Links |
| Bias | Rank |
| Up-to-date | Results |

| | |
|---|---|
| Search engine | Presentation |
| Sponsored links | Slideshow |
| Console | Balanced |
| Hyperlink | Interview |
| Interactive presentation | News reporting |
| Menu bar | Script |

Module 1 Finding and presenting information

| Sound recording software | Specialist software |
|---|---|
| | |
| | |
| | |
| | |
| | |

| | |
|---|---|
| Clarity | Upload |
| Design | Web page |
| Navigate | Website |
| Navigation | Browser |
| Tab | Code |
| Thumbnail | HTML |

# MODULE 2 KEYWORDS

| | |
|---|---|
| Html format | Mozilla |
| Mark-up language | Notepad |
| Specialist software | Tags |
| Standard software | Text editor |
| Browser | Button |
| Internet Explorer | Styles |

# MODULE 2 KEYWORDS

| Themes | Random |
|---|---|
| Website structure | Tabs |
| Application form | Tree |
| Linear | Website section |
| Online form | Wizard |
| Online shopping | |

# MODULE 3 KEYWORDS

| | |
|---|---|
| Predictions | If statements |
| Rules | Realistic |
| Variables | Absolute cell reference |
| What if | Relative cell reference |
| Accurate | Table |
| Drop-down lists | Text labels |

| | |
|---|---|
| Investment | Nested If Statement |
| Real-life | RANDBETWEEN |
| Simulation | Random numbers |
| Variables | |
| Conditional formatting | |
| | |

| | |
|---|---|
| Database software | Form |
| Data capture | Online form |
| Data collection | Police National Computer database |
| Data structure | Query |
| Field length | Table |
| Field size | Drop-down lists |

| | |
|---|---|
| Computer-based forms | Complex query |
| Online forms | Criteria |
| Paper-based forms | Criterion |
| Tick boxes | Greater than |
| User-friendly | Greater than or equal to |
| BETWEEN | Less than |

Module 4 Data handling

| | |
|---|---|
| Less than or equal to | Integrating |
| Query | Report |
| Simple query | Report heading |
| Columnar | Tabular |
| Integrated | |

| | |
|---|---|
| Bluetooth | Precision |
| Chip | Program |
| Computer microchip | Programmed |
| Error messages | Real-life situations |
| Memory card | Subroutine |
| Wireless connection | Counter |

| | |
|---|---|
| Efficient instructions | Control system |
| Inefficient instructions | Monitoring |
| Loop | Monitoring and Control system |
| Big Brother | System failure |
| | |
| | |

DL *DYNAMIC LEARNING* © Hodder Education 2008

| | |
|---|---|
| Anti-phishing software | Password |
| Data misuse | Personal data/information |
| Data Protection Act | Phishing |
| Data Protection Registrar | Sensitive data/information |
| Firewall | Spyware |
| Identity (ID) theft | Health and Safety |

**Module 6 Wider aspects of ICT**

| | |
|---|---|
| Health and Safety Policy | Downloading |
| Physical injury | Plagiarism |
| Physical strain | Research |
| RSI (Repetitive strain injury) | Computer technician |
| Stress | Digital divide |
| Copyright | Employment |

| | |
|---|---|
| ICT access | Developed countries |
| Redundant | Developing countries |
| Workplace | Newly industrialised countries |
| | |
| | |
| | |

| | |
|---|---|
| Forecast | Stock database |
| Keypad | Supercomputer |
| Prediction | User interface |
| Self-service kiosk | Visual display |
| | |
| | |

# SELF REVIEW SHEET

| Changes I have made to my work | How this has improved my work |
| --- | --- |
| | |
| | |
| | |
| | |
| | |

# PEER REVIEW SHEET

**Name of pupil who has done the work:**

**Your name:**

**Two things I liked and why.**

**One thing I would change and why.**

**Starter Activity** (Suggested answers)

You should view the Module 1 Case Study before you try these activities.

1  What sources of information are available to use if you wanted to find out about an important issue like global warming?

> *Internet sources: news items, pressure groups, government websites, scientific research*
> *Books, magazines, newspapers*
> *Interviews with experts*
> *Interviews with members of the public*

2  If you were using the Internet to find information, which search engine would you use and why?

> *Google, Ask Jeeves (Kids), AltaVista, Yahoo, Metacrawler, etc.*
> *Choice of search engine could be based on the coverage of the Internet or on popularity. For example, most people use Google because it has become the most popular.*
> *Other search engines such as Ask Jeeves and Yahoo have categories so you can search within categories, which can be quicker.*
> *Ask Jeeves (Kids) allows the user to type in questions rather than keywords, which younger pupils might find helpful.*

3  How could you be sure that the information you found was valid?

> *Check the URL to see if it is a gov or an org or a com.*
> *Double-check the information with another source.*
> *Check the amount of advertising and pop-ups to see what kind of site it is.*
> *Is the site from a well-known organisation that can be trusted such as a charity or government website?*
> *Look at which sites link to and from it to see if they are reputable.*

4  How could you be sure that the information you found was not biased?

*You can use some of the same techniques above. You should also look at the purpose of the website. For example, is it trying to sell you something, or is it trying to get you to see a particular point of view.*

5  Explain the difference between a fact and an opinion. Give examples.

*A fact is a piece of information that can be checked and can be proved. An opinion is just one person's view of something. For example, England lost the Ashes in 2006 is a fact. England are rubbish at cricket is an opinion.*

6  How can you be sure that facts are true?

> *Double-check them with other sources.*
> *Check who is telling you the fact to see if they are trustworthy.*

7  If you were going to explain all of the issues to do with global warming to your classmates, how would you present the information? Why would you present it in this way?

*You could produce: some printed material such as a word processed report, or a desktop published article; a multimedia slideshow; a sound recording (like a podcast); a video.*

# 1.1

 **End of Unit Activity:** Evaluating information (Suggested answers)

**In this activity you need to:**

> **Use techniques for evaluating information on websites**
> **Work out whether a website is reliable**
> **Show that you can tell the difference between a fact and an opinion**

Read the following statements. Some of them are FACTS and some of them are OPINIONS.

**1** For each one, state whether you think it is a fact or an opinion.

**2** Find information from at least two websites that supports your answer. Copy and paste the relevant information into this document. Include the URL of the sites.

Statement 1: There will be people living on the moon by the year 2020.

*Opinion. Pupils should be looking for information from reputable sites, e.g. BBC science news, UK Government websites, NASA website, European Space Agency website, British National Space Centre website.*

Statement 2: The movie *Titanic* received the most Oscar awards ever.

*Fact. There are a number of sites that they could use including any of the news sites, e.g. BBC, Reuters, or online versions of film or media magazines such as The Guardian, Empire online, or online encyclopaedias such as Wikipedia.*

Statement 3: The best-selling music album in 2006 was *Eyes open* by Snow Patrol.

*Fact. There are a number of sites that they could use including any of the news sites, e.g. BBC, Reuters, or online versions of music or media magazines such as The Guardian, NME, or online encyclopaedias such as Wikipedia, or information from the record company e.g EMI.*

Statement 4: Most people download music illegally.

*Opinion. Pupils should be looking for information from reputable sites that will have an interest in this subject. These could include news sites and record companies (such as those listed earlier), online music download sites such as iTunes or online CD shops such as HMV or Play.*

# 1.2

 **Written Task:** Checking validity (Suggested answers)

Read the statements in the table below. Your task is to complete the table.

On a scale of 1 to 3 rate how valid you think the information is:

  1 = Valid (you trust the information to be true)
  2 = Not sure
  3 = Invalid (you do NOT trust the information to be true)

Explain your rating in each case.

The first one has been done for you.

| Statement | Source | Rating (1, 2 or 3) | Reason |
|---|---|---|---|
| 'Poverty kills 50,000 people every day.' | Oxfam website | 1 | Oxfam is a well-known and trusted charity. |
| 'We offer the cheapest holidays on the Internet.' | Holiday company website | 2 or 3 | *They might be saying that just to get you to book a holiday. If they were a large well-known company it might be more trustworthy.* |
| 'Britain's biggest supermarket group is Tesco.' | BBC Business news website | *1* | *BBC is a well-known website for news and the information sounds plausible.* |
| 'Man never landed on the moon – it was a fake.' | Conspiracy forum | 2 or 3 | *The information could have come from anyone as it is from a forum. Also, the forum is where people can talk about conspiracies so will attract people with these views.* |
| '79% of the UK population has a mobile phone.' | Office of National Statistics | *1* | *This is a government website and its information is based on surveys.* |
| 'We are the best university in the UK if you want to study Law.' | University website | 2 or 3 | *They might be saying that just to get you to go to their university. It might be true but you would need some evidence to back it up – perhaps exam results.* |

DL DYNAMIC LEARNING © Hodder Education 2008

# 1.3

 **Practical Task:** Search engines (Suggested answers)

**1** The search engine I normally use is:

**2** I use this search engine because:

**3** You will need to find out information about each of these search engines. Then complete this table:

| Name of search engine | Why I might use it instead of my usual search engine |
|---|---|
| www.google.co.uk | *Currently the most popular and claims to have the best coverage.* |
| www.altavista.com | *They say that they are always creating new methods of searching to keep up-to-date with the information that changes on web pages.* |
| www.ajkids.com | *This is designed specifically for children and has a friendly design. It has categories so you can search within a category e.g. just search for a dictionary definition.* |
| www.yahoo.com | *Yahoo is organised into categories, which means you can browse as well as search. It has a kids only version.* |
| www.metacrawler.com | *This search engine searches Google, Yahoo, MSN Search and Ask and lists the results from all of them. This means that you can do one search and it will use four search engines to come up with the results.* |

**4** Two other search engines not listed above that I could use are:

1 *Yahoo!Kids, MSN Live, Dogpile, Webcrawler, All the web, Excite, Lycos, Ask*

2

# 1.3

Write down which keyword or keywords you would use to find the following information. You should try to get the most relevant sites listed at the top of the results. You should write it exactly as you would type it into a search engine.

*Students should be demonstrating an understanding that carefully chosen keywords with the use of speech marks and the + key will return relevant results, with a better chance that what they want will appear in the first page or two of results.*

**1** You want to buy a black printer cartridge for your OKI printer.
*"black printer cartrdidge" + OKI*

**2** You want to find out how to get from London to Manchester on a train.
*"train services" + London + Manchester*

**3** You want to find out when Elizabeth I was queen.
*"Elizabeth I" + reign*

**4** You want to know who is nominated for the Oscar for best actress this year.
*"Best actress" + nominations + 2008*

**5** You want to know the meaning of the word: Serendipity.
*define: serendipity*

**6** You want to know where the Dandenongs are.
*Dandenongs*

**7** You want to find the opening times of your local leisure centre.
*"Waterwings Leisure Centre" + "opening times"*

**8** You want to listen to a free radio station broadcast over the Internet.
*"free radio stations"*

# 1.5

 **Written Task:** News reports (Suggested answers)

Listen to the two radio reports about the use of incinerators. The scripts from each article are also available in the News Report 1 and News Report 2 documents.

Now answer these questions.

**1** One of these reports is biased and one is unbiased.

   **a** Which script is biased?       ~~Script 1~~ / Script 2

   **b** Which script is unbiased?    Script 1 / ~~Script 2~~

**2** Identify two biased statements contained in the biased report. Write them here.

*The UK really is becoming the "dirty man of Europe".*
*"People simply don't want the pollution and waste of resources that these monsters will bring".*

**3** Describe why you think the unbiased report gives a fairer picture of the issue.

*The unbiased report includes an equal number of arguments from both sides and summarises the main arguments of both. It does not give an opinion of its own or reach a conclusion, but leaves the debate open.*

**4** Identify two arguments in favour of incineration and two arguments against. Write them here.

*Arguments for:*
*Incinerators generate jobs for local people.*
*They generate electricity.*

*Arguments against:*
*They can cause traffic congestion and pollution.*
*They discourage people from recycling.*

# 2

## ☞ **Starter Activity** (Suggested answers)

You should view the Module 2 Case Study before you try these activities.

Select two websites and answer the following questions.

**1** What is the purpose and the audience for the website?

*The purpose will be to inform, persuade or entertain. Pupils may describe the audience in terms of age or gender.*

**2** What do you think about the design of the website?

*Pupils should comment on the layout of the pages, the consistency of design across pages, the use of fonts and colours, the use of images.*

**3** How have they made it easy for you to find what you want on the website?

*Pupils should comment on the ease of navigation: how easy it is to link from one page to another; whether there is a search facility; whether there is a site map; whether there are consistent design features such as buttons or tabs on each page.*

**4** How can you link to other pages within the website?

*Hyperlinks on text and images, use of buttons, use of tabs.*

**5** What software or tools can you use to create a website?

*HTML, Word, Publisher, FrontPage, Dreamweaver.  Pupils may also list other web-based tools.*

**6** Why might you choose one method of creating a website rather than another?

> *Ease of use*
> *Availability of software*
> *Cost of software*
> *Level of experience with software*
> *The features of the software, e.g. Dreamweaver has more features*
> *How complex the website is going to be*

# 2.1

 **Practical Task:** Purpose and audience (Suggested answers)

Visit the websites listed below and then complete the table. The first one has been done for you.

| Website | Purpose | Audience |
| --- | --- | --- |
| www.nspcc.org.uk | To inform you about the work of the charity.<br>To persuade you to get involved or make a donation. | General audience though there are sections just for children. |
| www.channel5.co.uk | *To inform you about what programmes are on Channel 5.*<br>*To persuade you to watch Channel 5.*<br>*To entertain you by showing programmes online.* | *Anyone who might be interested in watching Channel 5, which could be adults or children.* |
| www.hodderheadline.co.uk | *To inform you about what books they have for sale.*<br>*To persuade you to buy a book.* | *Mainly for adults as most of the books are for an adult audience.* |
| www.aqa.org.uk | *To inform teachers about subjects and exams.* | *Mainly for teachers.* |
| www.tesco.com | *To inform you about what products and services they sell.*<br>*To persuade you to buy them.* | *Mainly adults as they are the ones who usually do the shopping.* |
| http://kids.yahoo.com/ | *To entertain you.* | *Children.* |

DL DYNAMIC LEARNING © Hodder Education 2008

# 2.1

## Written Task: Web page design (Suggested answers)

1 Explain all of the ways in which you think the LifeBytes website has been designed to appeal to its audience.

*Use of bright primary colours.*
*Use of cartoon style graphics that would appeal to a young audience.*
*Use of more cartoon style fonts.*
*Use of large fonts, particularly on the links.*
*Not too much text, and lots of empty space.*
*Big clear links, e.g. the home button*

2 What is the purpose and audience for the Teachers' page?

*The audience is the teachers of the children who are visiting the LifeBytes website.*
*The purpose is to inform them of what is available on the site and how it can help the children.*

3 Explain which parts of the design have changed and which have stayed the same?

*The logo has stayed in the same place.*
*The name of the page has stayed in the same place.*
*The basic design of the web page is the same with the main links on the left hand side.*
*The background colour has stayed the same.*

*There is more text on the page and links within the text to other websites.*
*Fewer images have been used.*
*The links in the top right corner have been removed as users have to go back to the Teachers' home page to navigate to other pages.*

# 2.2

 **Practical Task:** Comparing methods (Suggested answers)

Your task is to create the web page about horses shown in the HTML worksheet. You will use Microsoft Word and then Microsoft Publisher to create the same page.

When you have made the web pages using both methods, answer these questions.

**1** Which method of creating the web page did you prefer and why?

*Pupils can make an independent choice here about which method they preferred, but it is important that their reasons are clearly stated. For example, Publisher may be preferred in terms of ease of positioning the text, line and image on the screen. Word may be preferred, as students may not like working with frames.*

**2** Describe any problems you had using either program to create your web page.

*Problems they might encounter:*

*In Publisher:*

*The standard page set up is not wide enough so the green background does not cover the whole screen in web preview.*
*There is no easy way to set a background colour – you have to draw on a rectangle and then fill it with colour.*
*When you put the text frames on you have to set the background colour to green or no fill otherwise they appear white.*
*It is not easy to change the heading that appears in the blue bar across the top of the browser.*
*Several files are created in a separate folder when the web page is published.*

*In Word:*

*It is quite difficult to position the text, line and image without the objects repositioning themselves.*
*It is not easy to change the heading that appears in the blue bar across the top of the browser.*
*Several files are created in a separate folder when the web page is published.*

**3** If a friend asked you which is the best way to produce a web page, which of these two methods would you recommend and why?

*Again, the student needs to make an independent choice here and their reasons may include some of the issues above. They may also include issues such as the software costs and availability, level of expertise with the software, and how long it takes to create pages.*

DL DYNAMIC LEARNING © Hodder Education 2008

# 2.2

## Written Task: HTML (Suggested answers)

(For the web page and the source code refer to the pupil activity worksheet on the Dynamic Learning CD-ROM.)

1. ```
   <HTML>
   <Head>
   <Title> I love horses </title>
   </head>
   ```

   What does this section of HTML code do?

   *Puts the text "I love horses" in the blue bar across the top of the browser window.*

2. ```
   <body bgcolor = "green">
   ```

   What does this section of HTML code do?

   *Sets the background colour of the page to green.*

3. ```
   <p align = "centre">
   <font face = "Arial" size = "10">Welcome to my horse page</font>
   </p>
   <hr>
   ```

   What does this section of HTML code do?

   *Sets the font style to Arial, centres the text and sets it to font size 10.*
   *Puts the text "Welcome to my horse page" on the screen.*
   *Draws a horizontal line under the text.*

4. ```
   <p>
   <font face = "Times New Roman" size = "4">My hobby is horse riding.
   <br/>Here is a picture of my horse.<b> Barnie </b></font>
   </p>
   ```

   What does this section of HTML code do?

   *Sets the font style to Times and sets the font size to 4.*
   *Puts the text "My hobby is horse riding" and "Here is a picture of my horse Barnie" on the screen on two lines.*
   *Puts the word "Barnie" in bold.*

5. ```
   <centre>
   <img src = "horse.bmp" alt = "My lovely horse"></img>
   </centre>
   ```

   What does this section of HTML code do?

   *Inserts the picture on the page.*
   ```

# 2.5

 **Written Task:** Website structures (Suggested answers)

Your task is to draw a clearly labelled diagram for each situation below to show how you would structure the websites.

## ● Website 1

A primary school wants a website with a home page that links to separate pages for each class from Year 1 to Year 6.

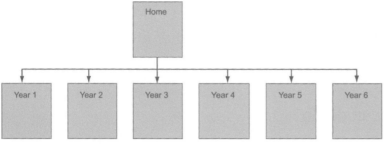

**Figure 1** A primary school website

## ● Website 2

A hotel wants a section of its website where customers can make a booking online. There will be three pages: Personal details, Booking details, Payment details. The customer must fill in the details on all of the pages.

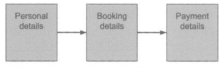

**Figure 2** A hotel website

## ● Website 3

A pop band wants a website with five pages: Home, Picture gallery, Biography, Tour dates and Reviews.

*Random or Linear would be suitable here. Random structure shown.*

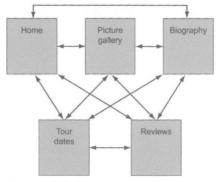

**Figure 3** A pop band website

# 3

 **Starter Activity** (Suggested answers)

You should view the Module 3 Case Study before you try these activities.

**1** Describe three examples where real-life situations are recreated on a computer.

*The question is about any model or simulation and NOT specifically about spreadsheet models. Therefore, pupils may list computer games that they have played, for example, simulation games such as The Sims, Theme Hospital, SimCity, etc. or games such as driving and fighting games. They may list more useful applications such as flight simulators for training pilots, or models to predict the weather. Some pupils may list spreadsheet models that they created in InteraCT 1, e.g. financial models.*

**2** What are the advantages of using a computer to model real-life situations?

> *Can be cheaper than doing it in real life.*
> *Can be safer than doing it in real life.*
> *You can carry out 'what if' scenarios to predict what might happen without having to do it for real.*
> *Computer models allow you to experience things that you might not get the chance to in real life.*
> *You can make mistakes on the computer before you try things in real life.*
> *You can recreate situations that might take a long time in real life.*

**3** What are the disadvantages of using a computer to model real-life situations?

> *Computer models are never as realistic as doing something for real.*
> *Unexpected factors might mean that things happen differently in real life.*

**4** Spreadsheets are used to create models. Describe two examples of how a spreadsheet model could be used in real life.

> *Examples could be anything that involves an element of prediction or a 'what if' capability:*
> >*Predicting the number of sales in a shop*
> >*Predicting levels of profit*
> >*Predicting how many people might attend an event*
> >*Working out how many people can go on a school trip.*

**5** Why might graphs be useful when looking at a spreadsheet model?

> *Graphs can help people to visualise data.*
> *They are a good way of summarising complex data.*
> *They are a good way of summarising large amounts of data.*

**6** How realistic do you think computer models are?

*This depends on how they were built. If they include all the possible variables and if the data and rules that go into building them are accurate and realistic then there is no reason why they should not recreate real life quite accurately.*

# 3.1

 **Written Task:** Identifying variables (Suggested answers)

Your task is to identify what variables you would need to use in a spreadsheet model, if you were trying to solve these problems. The first one has been done for you.

**1** A clothes shop wants to predict the total amount of money it will make from selling clothes.

*Variables needed:*
> *The items they sell, e.g. Jeans, tops, etc.*
> *The price of each item*
> *The number of each item sold*

**2** A student wants to predict the total cost of running a car for a year.

*Variables needed:*
> *The cost of the car*
> *Cost of petrol*
> *The number of miles he/she expects to travel*
> *Running costs, such as new tyres, repairs and maintenance*
> *Cost of insurance*
> *Cost of breakdown cover*

**3** A concert hall wants to predict how much profit it will make putting on a pop concert.

*Variables needed:*
> *How much the pop band will be paid*
> *Cost of advertising the concert*
> *Cost of heating and lighting the hall*
> *Cost of the staff in the hall*
> *How many people they predict will come to the concert*
> *How much each ticket will be*

**4** A school wants to predict what grades pupils will get in their English, Maths and Science SATs exams.

*Variables needed:*
> *The name of the pupil*
> *The subject*
> *Their previous grades*
> *Their current level of effort*

**5** NASA wants to predict how much fuel they need to send a rocket to Mars.

*Variables needed:*
> *Distance to Mars*
> *The weight of the rocket*
> *The number of kilometres the rocket will travel per litre of fuel*

# 3.1

*Also see the Concert Hall Evacuation Model (Suggested solution) Excel file.*

A large concert hall has seating for 3000 people. They want to know how quickly they could get everyone out of the hall if there was a fire.

They know that they can evacuate 100 people per minute out of each fire exit. At the moment, they have three fire exits in the hall.

Your task is to create a spreadsheet model to solve this problem and then answer the following questions.

1 How many minutes would it take to evacuate the hall if there were 3000 people in it? *10 minutes*

2 How many minutes would it take to evacuate the hall if there were 2000 people in it? *6.67 minutes*

3 They are thinking about building an extra fire exit. How many minutes would it take to evacuate the hall of 3000 people with this extra fire exit? *7.5 minutes*

4 Their health and safety officer tells them that they need to be able to evacuate 3000 people in 3 minutes. How many fire exits do they need? *10 fire exits.*

5 How accurate do you think your model is? What other variables could you build in to make it more realistic?

*Pupils may comment on the following:*

> *The only way to test the accuracy of the calculations would be to carry out a real evacuation.*

> *People may actually move much quicker in the event of a real emergency.*

*There may be other variables that should be considered. For example:*

> *They may consider the impact of the age and mobility of the audience. Old or disabled people may not be able to leave as quickly as others.*

> *They may take into account the possibility that the fire is blocking one or more of the exits.*

> *They may take into account poor visibility through smoke in the event of a real fire.*

> *They may take into account the amount of time it takes for people to register that it is a real fire alarm and not a test. (Many people assume that the alarm is a test and wait until someone asks them to leave).*

# 3.2

 **Written Task:** Checking a model (Suggested answers)

Your task is to review the Mobile Phone model that we used in the last unit.

Look at the model below and then answer the questions:

| | A | B | C | D |
|---|---|---|---|---|
| 1 | Mobile Phone Model | | | |
| 2 | | | | |
| 3 | Charges | Amount | Predicted number over one year | Totals |
| 4 | Price of phone | £ 89.99 | - | £ 89.99 |
| 5 | Cost of texts | £ 0.10 | 1800 | £ 180.00 |
| 6 | Cost of calls | £ 0.25 | 1000 | £ 250.00 |
| 7 | | | | |
| 8 | Total cost | | | £ 519.99 |
| 9 | | | | |

*Microsoft Excel - 3.2_A_Mobile Phone Model*
*File Edit View Insert Format Tools Data Window Help*
*G14*

**Figure 1** Spreadsheet used to check phone costs

1 How accurate do you think the model is? Explain your answer.

*Pupils may think that the model is not very accurate as it is difficult to predict the number of texts and calls that you are likely to make over a year. This means that the model only gives a very rough estimate of the total cost.*

2 How realistic do you think the model is? Explain your answer.

*Pupils may think that the model is not very realistic because:*
*It only seems to cover 'pay as you go' (PAYG) schemes and not contract options where you pay monthly.*
*Some phones are free when you sign up to a contract.*
*It does not include free texts and calls that you might get.*
*It does not include other charges such as Internet access.*
*It does not allow you to compare the features of the phone, for example whether it has a camera, music player, Internet access, etc.*

3 Describe what changes you would make to the model to make it more realistic.

*Suggested answers may include:*
*Look at the costs per month instead of per year so you can compare contract to PAYG.*
*Include contract options as well as PAYG.*
*Include something that lets you compare the features of the phones.*
*Include different tariffs from different networks.*

# 3.3

## Written Task: Setting up data (Suggested answers)

This exercise can be completed as a Practical Task or a Written Task.

The following data are recorded as part of a science experiment.

Pupils filled two containers with boiling water. One container was insulated and the other was not. They wanted to compare how quickly the temperature changed in the two containers. They recorded the temperature in each container every 30 seconds. They took ten readings.

The results (in Celsius) were:

Container 1: 100, 97, 95, 93, 91, 89, 88, 86, 84, 82

Container 2: 100, 97, 96, 95, 94, 93, 92, 91, 90, 89

## ● Task 1

Draw a diagram to show how you could set up these data as a table in a spreadsheet so that they could be graphed.

*Pupils may produce the actual results in a spreadsheet if they have access to a computer for this exercise.*

| Time (secs) | Container 1 temperature (Celsius) | Container 2 temperature (Celsius) |
|---|---|---|
| 30 | 100 | 100 |
| 60 | 97 | 97 |
| 90 | 96 | 96 |
| 120 | 93 | 95 |
| 150 | 91 | 94 |
| 180 | 89 | 93 |
| 210 | 88 | 92 |
| 240 | 86 | 91 |
| 270 | 84 | 90 |
| 300 | 82 | 89 |

## ● Task 2

Draw a rough design of the graph(s) you would produce to show these results.

*Pupils may produce the actual results in a spreadsheet if they have access to a computer for this exercise.*

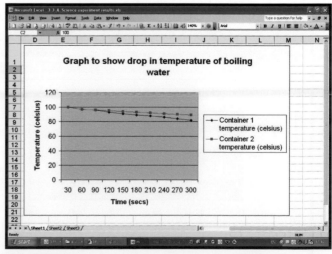

**Figure 1** Graph showing loss of heat in different containers

DL DYNAMIC LEARNING © Hodder Education 2008

# 3.3

 **End of Unit Activity:** Graphing data (Suggested answers)

**In this activity you need to:**

> **Use graphs to answer 'what if' type questions**
> **Set up data for plotting**
> **Select the data to plot**

Your task is to create suitable graphs using the '10km Running times' model. This shows how long it takes three different runners to run a 10km (6 miles) race. Their times are recorded for each kilometre.

**1** Create a graph or graphs to show the times at each 1km interval for all three runners. Copy and paste your graph here.

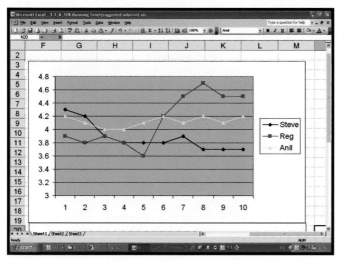

**Figure 1** Graph showing running times for each km

**2** Create a graph or graphs that will show the total time for the 10km race for each runner. Copy and paste your graph here.

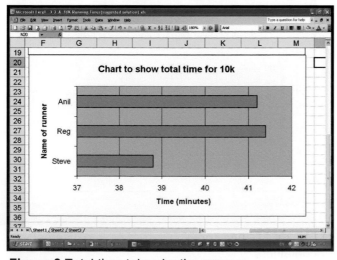

**Figure 2** Total time taken by the runners

Now use the graphs to answer the following questions:

3  Which runner is fastest over 10km? *Steve*

4  Which runner has the fastest time for any single kilometre? *Reg*

5  Who is the most consistent runner? That is, they have the smallest variation in how long it takes them to run each kilometre? *Anil*

6. Who do you think might win a 5km race based on these times? *Reg*

# 3.3

 **End of Unit Activity:** Graphing data (Suggested answers)

Your task is to create suitable graphs using the '10km Running times' model. This shows how long it takes three different runners to run a 10km (6 miles) race. Their times are recorded for each kilometre.

Your task is to create a suitable graph or graphs and use them to answer the following questions. Copy and paste your graphs at the end of this document.

Now use the graphs to answer the following questions:

1  Which runner is fastest over 10km? *Steve*

2  Which runner has the fastest time for any single kilometre? *Reg*

3  Who is the most consistent runner? That is, they have the smallest variation in how long it takes them to run each kilometre? *Anil*

4  Who do you think might win a 5km race based on these times? *Reg*

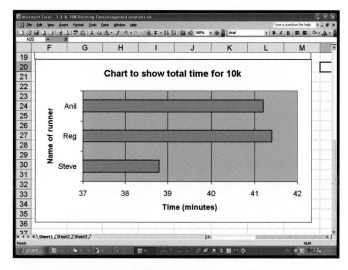

**Figure 1** Total running times

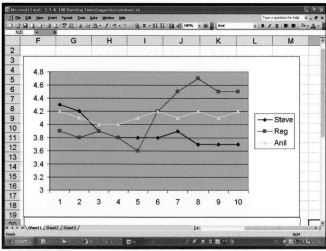

**Figure 2** Times for each km interval

# 3.4

 ## Written Task: Variables and rules (Suggested answers)

A **variable** is a factor that computer games have to take into account so that they are like real life. For example, in a flight simulator, they have to include weather conditions and what type of plane it is.

A **rule** is how the game decides what will happen depending on what instructions it gets from the player. For example, in a flight simulator, if the player pushes the accelerator, the plane must go faster.

Your task is to identify the variables and rules that might be used in the following computer games.

## 1 Formula 1 Racing Game

This game lets you build and then race your Formula 1 car. The objective is to win as many races as possible.

### Variables

*Type of car; Size of engine; Type of tyre; Which circuit; Weather conditions; Driver skill*

### Rules

*Pressing the accelerator makes the car go faster; Pressing the brake makes the car go slower; Turning the wheel makes the car turn in the same direction; You have to start in first gear; The higher the gear, the faster the car will go; If you skid, the car slows down; If you crash, you are out of the race*

## 2 Raise your own Pet

This game lets you buy and look after your own pet. The objective is to win awards in pet shows.

### Variables

*Cost of the pet; Cost of feeding; Vet's bills; Amount of time spent training the pet; Amount of time spent grooming the pet*

### Rules

*The more you spend on the pet, the more likely it is to win awards; The more time you spend grooming your pet, the more likely it is to win awards; If you neglect your pet, it gets ill; It you train your pet, it is more likely to win an award*

DL DYNAMIC LEARNING © Hodder Education 2008

# 3.4

 **End of Unit Activity:** Understanding Investment Manager (Suggested answers)

You will need to experiment with the Investment Manager spreadsheet before you answer these questions.

Remember that the objective of Investment Manager is to make as much money as possible over five years.

**1** Which of the four options is likely to **make** you the most money over five years?

*Savings Account*

**2** Which of the four options is likely to **lose** you the most money over five years?

*Gambling*

**3** If you had £10,000 to invest, how would you split it across the four options and why?

*Pupils may give different answers. The way the model is made, the pupils should conclude that the Savings Account produces the largest returns on average over a five year period. However, they may suggest that they take a higher risk in Year 1 (e.g. Stock market) and then take a lower risk in later years. The Stock market and Gambling both offer the possibility of higher rewards.*

**4** What is the most money you have **made** playing Investment Manager? Copy and paste your best ever result here. What did you set as the options to get this result?

*Pupils will copy and paste their own answers here. The model is built with random numbers so the results will be different for every pupil.*

**5** What is the most money you have **lost** playing Investment Manager?. Copy and paste your worst ever result here. What did you set as the options to get this result?

*Pupils will copy and paste their own answers here. The model is built with random numbers so the results will be different for every pupil.*

**6** Describe what calculations you think the model is using to predict the results.

*Pupils should identify that the values typed into the first worksheet (Set up Investments) are multiplied by a percentage to generate the values on the second worksheet (Results).*

*They may identify that the safer investments (Savings Account and Premium Bonds) never produce a negative return although the amount they will*

 © Hodder Education 2008

*generate is limited. They may identify that the last two options (Stock Market and Gambling) can produce high results, but there is less chance of this.*

*More able pupils will identify that random numbers are being used to generate the results.*

*More able pupils will identify that the results are cumulative i.e. that the results of Year 2 are based on the results of Year 1 and so on.*

**7** Do you think the model is realistic? If not, what other factors would you add to it?

*Pupils may not be able to comment on the realism in terms of the actual values but they should identify that the results are broadly realistic i.e. gambling is much more risky than a savings account, but there is the occasional chance that you could get lucky.*

*They may think of other variables that need adding in such as further investment options, for example buying and selling property or goods.*

*They may identify that in real life you could keep an eye on your investments and make changes as the year progresses.*

# 3.5

**Written Task:** Random numbers (Suggested answers)

## ● Question 1

The National Lottery main draw uses balls numbered 1 to 49. They are drawn at random.

22  26  38  39  41  42    08

A spreadsheet is used to simulate the draw of the six balls and the bonus ball.

This formula is used: RANDBETWEEN (0-49).

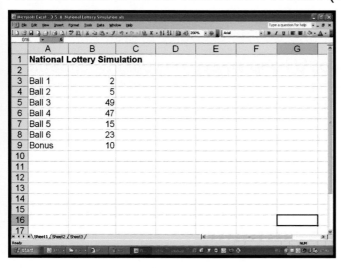

**Figure 1** Balls drawn in the National Lottery

The simulation is then run:

**a** The first number the simulation comes up with is 49. Is this realistic?

*Yes.*

**b** The next number the simulation comes up with is 0. Is this realistic?

*No, because there is not a 0 ball in the lottery.*

**c** The next number the simulation comes up with is 49 again. Is this realistic?

*No, because once the 49 has been drawn, it is no longer in the machine and cannot be drawn again.*

**d** There is an equal chance of getting any number from 1 to 49. Is this realistic?

*Yes. There should be an equal chance of getting any of the numbers.*

# ● Question 2

A standard dartboard has the numbers 1–20.

The bullseye is worth 50 and the ring around the bullseye is worth 25.

You can also score doubles and trebles of any of the numbers from 1–20.

A spreadsheet is used to simulate the score that someone might get throwing one dart.

This formula is used: RANDBETWEEN (1-60).

**Figure 2**

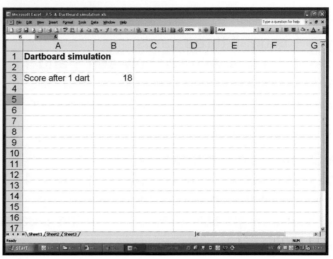

**Figure 3** Scoring at darts

The simulation is then run:

**a** The first number the simulation comes up with is 20. Is this realistic?

*Yes.*

**b** The next number the simulation comes up with is 23? Is this realistic?

*No. It is not possible to score 23 as the numbers only go up to 20 and then there are doubles and trebles, but none of them equal 23.*

**c** Sometimes a player misses the board completely. How could you change the formula to take account of this?

*Change it to RANDBETWEEN (0-60).*

**d** There is an equal chance of getting any of the numbers from 1 to 60. Is this realistic?

*Probably not in real life. Good players will get higher scores on average. Bad players will get lower scores. It is harder to hit a treble than it is to hit a double or a single, so these should come out of the simulation less often.*

# 3.5

 **End of Unit Activity:** Card game simulation (Suggested answers)

Your task is to create a card game based on the game Blackjack (also known as twenty ones).

The rules are:

> Player 1 is dealt three cards.
> Each card has a value of between 1 and 11.
> The value of the three cards is added up.
> If the value is greater than 21 then Player 1 is bust and the Dealer wins.

If the value is 21 or less:

> The Dealer is dealt three cards.
> Each card has a value of between 1 and 11.
> The value of the three cards is added up.
> If the value is greater than 21 then the Dealer is bust and Player 1 wins.

If neither Player 1 nor the Dealer is bust:

> Whoever has the highest number wins.
> If they have the same value, the Dealer wins.

**Your task**

1  Create a model that can be used to simulate this card game.

2  Add any conditional formatting or If statements to make it clear who has won each time the simulation is run.

   *See the Card game simulation (Suggested solutions) file.*

3  Why might your model not be 100% realistic?

   *The system deals three cards. In real life you can choose how many cards you want and whether to stick or twist.*

   *There is a greater chance of getting a 10 than the other numbers as jacks, queens and kings are all worth 10. Therefore, you are three times more likely to get a 10 than any of the other numbers. The random number assumes an equal chance of getting any of the numbers.*

# 4

You should view the Module 4 Case Study before you try these activities.

**1** What is a database?

*A collection of data on a related topic.*

**2** What are databases used for?

> *Databases are used to store data.*
> *Databases can be analysed to find things out.*
> *Databases can be searched and sorted to look for particular information.*
> *Pupils might come up with specific examples of how organisations use databases at this point.*

**3** Who do you think might store your personal details in a database?

*Doctor; Dentist; School; Hospital; Government; Clubs; Internet service provider; Email provider.*

**4** How do people collect the information that is stored on a database?

*Questionnaire; Form; Automatically, e.g. when people use their credit cards.*

**5** Why might some people be worried about having their personal information stored on a database?

> *Businesses might sell your information to other businesses, which means you might get lots of junk mail or junk email.*

> *Criminals might get hold of your details and steal them.*
> *Criminals might buy something using your credit card.*
> *People might get hold of information that you want to keep personal such as health information.*

**6** What software could you use to make a database?

> *Spreadsheet software, e.g. Excel*
> *Database software, e.g. Access, PinPoint, ViewPoint, FlexiDATA*

**7** Give examples of what these organisations might use databases for:

**a** The police
   > *Storing details about criminals and the crimes they have committed.*
   > *Identifying who might have committed a crime.*
   > *Storing details about cars and drivers.*
**b** Your doctor
   > *Sending out reminders for check-ups or injections.*
   > *Sharing the details with other medical people such as the hospital.*
**c** An online shop
   > *Storing personal details so that goods can be sent to the right address.*
   > *Analysing the database to see which products are the most or least popular.*
   > *Creating a mailing list to send people details of special offers.*

# 4.1

 **Written Task:** Designing a data structure (Suggested answers)

Your task is to create the **data structure** for a concert ticket database.

The database is being created for a business that sells concert tickets over the Internet.

Complete the table below. The first two fields have been done for you. You need to think carefully about what data needs to be collected.

| Field name | Data type | Length / Options | Validation check |
|---|---|---|---|
| Title | Multiple choice / List | 4 options: Mr, Mrs, Ms or Miss | Must select one of the four answers |
| Name | Text | 30 characters | Must be answered |
| Address | Text | 100 characters (or split over several lines e.g. Address 1, Address 2, Town, Postcode) | Must be answered |
| Date of concert | Date | DD/MM/YYYY | Must answer in date format |
| Name of band / concert | Text | 30 characters | Must be answered |
| Number of tickets wanted | Number | 2 digits | Range check between 0 and 10 |
| Price per ticket | Number / Currency | 4 digits (£00.00) | Range check between £0.00 and £99.99 |
| Total price | Number / Currency | 5 digits (£000.00) | Range check between £0.00 and £999.99 |
| Payment method | Multiple Choice / List | 3 options: Credit Card, Debit Card, PayPal | Must select one of the three options Must be answered |

# 4.2

 **Written Task:** Designing a form (Suggested answers)

Your task is to design a **form** for the concert ticket database that you set up in the last unit.

Your form should:

> Have a suitable layout
> Include all of the fields
> Be as easy for people to fill in as possible
> Allow enough space for people to type in their information
> Provide instructions on how to fill the form in if needed.

*Their design may be hand-drawn or produced on the computer. Pupils should:*

> *Include all the fields listed in their table*
> *Create an easy-to-use layout*
> *Use appropriate fonts and colours*
> *Provide drop-down lists and option boxes where relevant*
> *Provide instructions for the person filling in the form*
> *Leave enough space for answers.*

# 4.3

## Written Task: Writing queries (Suggested answers)

This is part of the Dog Rescue database. Write out the queries that are needed to get the following information. For example, to list all dogs that are grey the query would need to be: Colour = "Grey"

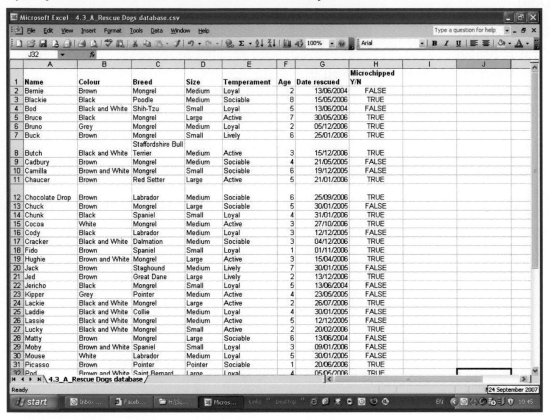

**Figure 1** Dog Rescue database

**1** List all dogs that are black and white. *Colour = "Black and White"*

**2** List all dogs that are black or white. *Colour = "Black" OR "White"*

**3** List all dogs that have NOT been microchipped. *Microchipped = "No"*

**4** List all dogs that are less than 6 years olds. *Age <6*

**5** List all dogs that are 6 years old or less. *Age <=6*

**6** List all dogs that are aged between 3 and 6. *Age BETWEEN 3 and 6*

**7** List all dogs that are medium or large. *Size = "Medium" OR "Large"*

**8** List all dogs that have been rescued since 1st January 2006. *Date rescued >= 01/01/2006*

**9** List all dogs that are large and are 2 years old or younger. *Size = "Large" AND Age <=2*

**10** List all dogs that are large and are 2 years old or older. *Size = "Large" AND Age >=2*

# 4.3

 **End of Unit Activity:** Querying the Dog Rescue database (Suggested answers)

Use the Dog Rescue database to find the answer to these questions.

1 How many dogs are there on the database? *50*

2 How many mongrels are there? *21*

3 How many dogs are 3 years old? *10*

4 How many dogs are 8 years old or older? *1*

5 How many dogs are between 3 and 5 years old? *27*

6 How many dogs less than 3 years old have been microchipped? *9*

7 How many dogs are less than 3 years old and are loyal? *5*

8 How many dogs are loyal or sociable? *31*

9 How many dogs are small or medium sized? *38*

10 How many dogs are Spaniels or Labradors? *8*

# 4.3

 **End of Unit Activity:** Querying the Dog Rescue database (Suggested answers)

Use the Dog Rescue database to find the answer to these questions.

1 How many dogs less than 3 years old have been microchipped? *9*

2 How many dogs are less than 3 years old and are loyal? *5*

3 How many dogs are loyal or sociable? *31*

4 How many dogs are small or medium sized? *38*

5 How many dogs are Spaniels or Labradors? *8*

Some people come to the rescue centre looking for a particular kind of dog. Which dogs would you suggest the following people might want to take home?

6 A young family want a sociable or loyal dog that is no more than 2 years old.

   *Bernie. Bruno, Fido, Picasso, Reggie, Scooby, Scrappy or Spencer.*

7 A young man wants a lively dog to take walking with him. He wouldn't mind an older dog (over 5 years old) but it must be microchipped.

   *Buck*

8 A couple want a Labrador, Red Setter or Great Dane. It must be microchipped.

   *Chaucer, Chocolate drop, Jed.*

9 An old lady wants a small dog. She is very charitable and will look at any of the dogs even if no-one else wants them. The dogs that no-one wants are the ones that have been at the rescue centre the longest.

   *Bod, Jericho or Scooby.*

10 A young girl wants a large, lively dog, preferably brown or brown and white.

   *Jed*

# 4.4

☞ **Practical Task:** Creating a report (Suggested answers)

This exercise follows on from the written exercise on report design.

Your task is to create the reports that you designed earlier. The scenarios are below as a reminder.

1 The vet is coming to the centre to fit microchips to all the dogs that need one. Design a report that would give the vet the information they need.

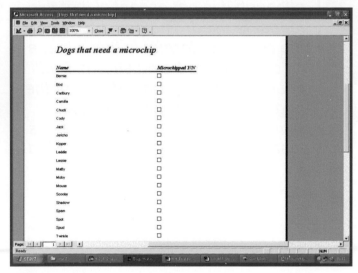

**Figure 1** Report showing dogs needing microchips

*The vet will only need the name of the dog for identification purposes so it is not really necessary to include any of the other fields.*

*The microchipped field has been included to confirm that they have NOT been microchipped.*

*The vet could use the report as a checklist as they work their way through the dogs.*

*The report would need to be printed so the vet could keep it with them while they were working.*

2 The manager is working out the dog-walking rota. All the lively dogs need walking three times a day. Design a report that can be given to the staff so they know which dogs to walk three times a day.

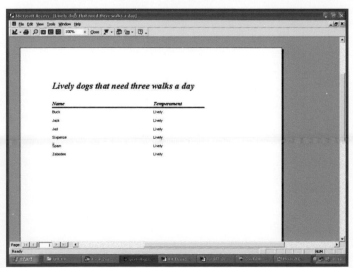

**Figure 2** Report showing lively dogs

*The staff only need to know the names of the dogs that need walking three times a day, so none of the other fields have been included.*

*The Temperament field has been printed for confirmation.*

*This report would probably be put up on a notice board or handed to the staff individually.*

**3** Some people contact the centre via email asking if they have dogs with certain characteristics, for example must be sociable, must be small, must be brown, etc. Design a report that could be emailed back listing all the dogs that fit their criteria.

**Figure 3** Report showing lively dogs

*This report needs to show all of the details for the dogs that fit the criteria. People looking for a dog will want to know all about it so they should be given as much information as possible.*

*This report is set out using the 'Columnar' option in Access, although it is not essential that this format is used. The advantage of the columnar format is that when a lot of fields are being shown, it will not go off the right-hand side of the page like the standard Tabular format. The important point here is that all the information is displayed.*

# 4.4

 **Written Task:** Designing a report (Suggested answers)

*The emphasis of this exercise is on the design (not the production) of the report. Pupils may create hand-drawn or computerised designs.*

*Suggested answers have been provided in the 'Creating reports' worksheet. Please see this file.*

The Dog Rescue database is used by lots of different people for different reasons.

For each situation below, design a report that would give them the information they need. You do not have to make the report at this stage, just design it.

1 The vet is coming to the centre to fit microchips to all the dogs that need one. Design a report that would give the vet the information they need.

2 The manager is working out the dog-walking rota. All the lively dogs need walking three times a day. Design a report that can be given to the staff so they know which dogs to walk three times a day.

3 Some people contact the centre via email asking if they have dogs with certain characteristics, for example must be sociable, must be small, must be brown, etc. Design a report that could be emailed back listing all the dogs that fit their criteria.

**End of Module Assignment:** Swimming gala
(Suggested answers)

Your task is to design and create a database to solve the following problem.

The school swimming gala takes place once a year. Your task is to create a database that can be used to record all of the details of the swimmers, the events they have entered and where they came in their race. You may collect other details that you think are relevant.

**1** Complete the table below to show how you will set up the database:

| Field Name | Data type | Length | Validation |
|---|---|---|---|
| Name | Text | 50 | Must be filled in |
| Gender | Text | 1 | Set as a drop down list e.g. M or F |
| Form | Text | 2 | Set as drop down list e.g. 7S, 7T, etc. |
| House | Text | 10 | Set as drop down list e.g. Blue, red, etc. |
| Event | Text | 20 | Set as drop down list e.g. 100m freestyle, 100m backstroke, etc. |
| Position | Number | 2 | Set a range check between 1 and 12 (or whatever the max number per event is) |
| Time | Date/Time | 6 digits | In the format 000.000 seconds |

**2** Create a form that can be used to fill in the details. Copy and paste it here.

*Form should include all of the fields listed above.*
*It should have a clear and easy-to-use layout.*
*It should have a title and perhaps some instructions on how to fill it in.*
*It should use drop down lists and tick boxes where possible to make it easier to fill in and less error-prone.*

**3** After the event, someone will be using the database to identify the 1st, 2nd and 3rd placed swimmer in each event. Explain how this can be done with your database.

*This will be done through the use of queries. They will need to query on the Event and the Position, e.g. Event = "100m freestyle" and Position = 1 or 2 or 3.*

**4** In the table above you have listed a number of fields. Explain how the school might be able to use these data.

*The school could use the data to find out:*
> *How many girls take part compared to boys*
> *Which year groups tend to have the most swimmers*
> *What the best ever time is for an event*
> *Which house had the most winners*
> *Which form had the most winners*
> *Pupils may have suggested other fields so this is not an exhaustive list.*

DL DYNAMIC LEARNING © Hodder Education 2008

# 5

 ## Starter Activity (Suggested answers)

You should view the Module 5 Case Study before you try these activities.

**1** List as many examples of computer control as you can.

> *Pupils may list household electronic devices such as:*
>> *Mobile phones, CD and DVD players/recorders, MP3 players, microwaves, alarm clocks, fridges, TVs, home cinema systems.*
> *Pupils may list devices on vehicles:*
>> *Sat Nav systems, parking sensors or cards, cruise control, engine management systems.*
> *Pupils may list devices in public spaces:*
>> *Automatic doors, heating and cooling systems, car park entry systems, toll booths, turnstiles, ticket machines.*
> *Pupils may list large-scale industrial and commercial systems:*
>> *Car manufacturing, aeroplane flight systems, space travel flight systems*

**2** What are the advantages of having computers controlling things for us?

*The main advantages are that they make our lives easier and safer.*

**3** What are the disadvantages of having computers controlling things for us?

*The main disadvantages are that the systems can fail or be misused.*

**4** In what ways can computer-controlled systems make our lives safer?

*Flight systems in aeroplanes; automatic electricity cut-off; temperature control in nuclear reactors.*

**5** What is the worse thing that could happen if a control system failed?

*In the worst case, the failure of the system could lead to death. For example if a flight system in an aeroplane failed, or a nuclear reactor exploded.*

**6** List examples of how you personally might be monitored by computer systems.

*CCTV recordings; number plate recognition on speed cameras; finger prints stored by the school, computer log-on detail and activities monitored by the technician; mobile phone use.*

**7** Why might some people not like being monitored by computer systems?

*They may think that it is an infringement of their privacy. This means that they do not like being monitored without knowing why it is happening, or what people might do with the information that they find out from monitoring.*

# 5.1

 **Written Task:** Writing control instructions (Suggested answer)

This is a Health Measurement Unit. You find them in leisure centres. They use sensors to measure your height, weight and blood pressure.

You stand on the machine, put your money or credit card in and grab the two handles. It automatically does all the measurements and prints out the results for you to take away.

It has audio instructions to tell the user what to do.

Your task is to write out the instructions that would be needed to control this machine.

*1 User stands on the machine.*

*2 Machine should sense that someone has stood on the machine and there should be a voice message telling them that they need to make payment, and how much payment is needed.*

*3 User selects whether they want to pay by cash or credit card.*

*4 User makes payment with cash or credit card.*

*5 Machine tells the user to grab the handles and stand still.*

*6 Sensors then take the readings: height, weight and blood pressure.*

*7 The machine creates the printout.*

*8 Machine tells the user to step off the machine and take the printout.*

*Pupils may also identify possible errors that could occur, such as the user not entering the correct money or not standing on the machine or not gripping the handles.*

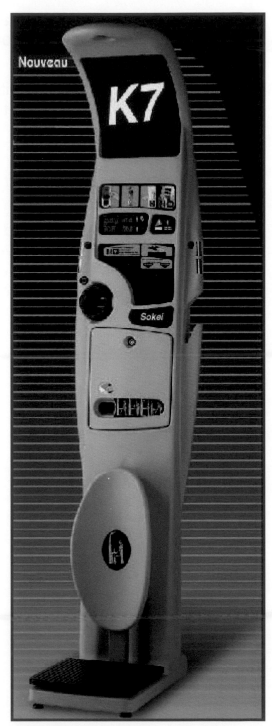

**Figure 1** A Health Measurement Unit

# 5.1

 **End of Unit Activity:** Creating a flowchart (Suggested answer)

Your task is to create the flowchart for the Health Measurement Unit that you wrote the instructions for earlier.

The flowchart should be as detailed as possible and include comments to explain each step.

*Suggested answer shown below. This answer is a L5 response. It shows working solutions with all the main steps.*

*A L6 student may go into more detail, for example, including the other payment options and explaining more about the sensors used to take the height, weight and blood pressure readings.*

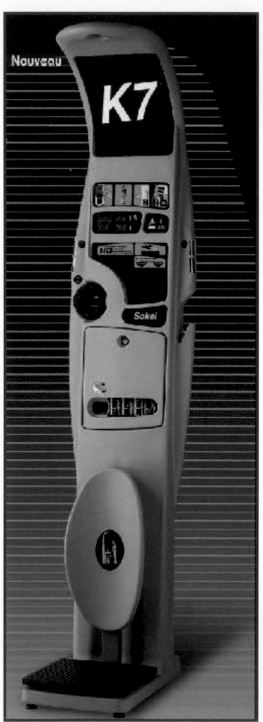

**Figure 1** A Health Measurement Unit

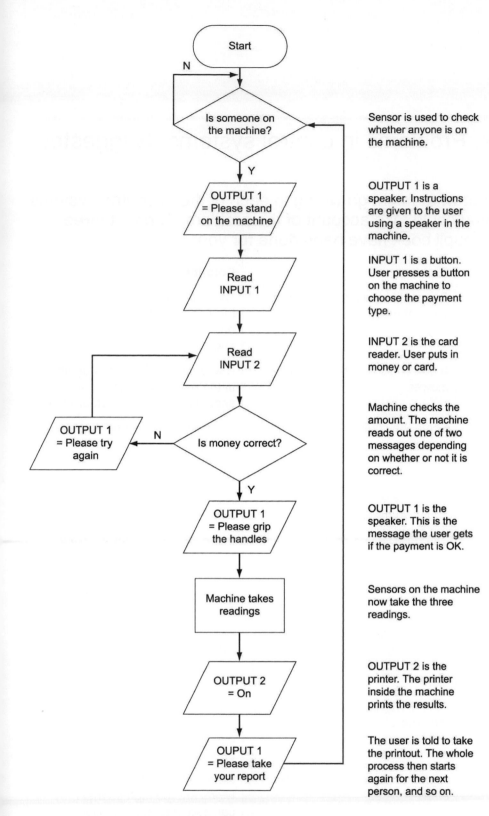

**Figure 2** Flowchart showing how to control the machine

The flowchart contains the following elements and annotations:

Start

**Is someone on the machine?** — Sensor is used to check whether anyone is on the machine. (N loops back; Y continues)

**OUTPUT 1 = Please stand on the machine** — OUTPUT 1 is a speaker. Instructions are given to the user using a speaker in the machine.

**Read INPUT 1** — INPUT 1 is a button. User presses a button on the machine to choose the payment type.

**Read INPUT 2** — INPUT 2 is the card reader. User puts in money or card.

**Is money correct?** — Machine checks the amount. The machine reads out one of two messages depending on whether or not it is correct. (N → OUTPUT 1 = Please try again; Y continues)

**OUTPUT 1 = Please try again**

**OUTPUT 1 = Please grip the handles** — OUTPUT 1 is the speaker. This is the message the user gets if the payment is OK.

**Machine takes readings** — Sensors on the machine now take the three readings.

**OUTPUT 2 = On** — OUTPUT 2 is the printer. The printer inside the machine prints the results.

**OUPUT 1 = Please take your report** — The user is told to take the printout. The whole process then starts again for the next person, and so on.

# 5.2

 **Written Task:** Problems in control systems (Suggested answers)

Your task is to think about what might go wrong in each of these control systems and then suggest how you could take account of the problem. The first three examples that are in the pupil book have been done for you.

| Control system | Problem | Solution |
|---|---|---|
| Car park barrier | Car could break down when it is under the barrier. | Use a sensor to check whether there is anything under the barrier. If there is, the barrier should not come down. |
| Robotic lawn mower | A dog could run in front of the mower. | Use a sensor. If there is anything in the path of the mower, it should change direction or stop. |
| Vending machine | Someone could put in the wrong money. | A message should be displayed asking for more money. It should not dispense the product until the correct money has been put in. |
| Burglar alarm | *The burglar could cut the power supply to the alarm.* | *Have a battery back-up system in case the power supply is cut.* |
| Fire alarm | *The batteries could go flat.* | *It should have a button on it to test whether there is any power in the battery.*<br><br>*It should beep when the battery power is low.* |
| Automatic door | *Small people or people in wheel chairs may not be picked up by the sensors and the doors will not open.* | *Add extra sensors at lower levels rather than just above the door.* |
| Microwave oven | *People might forget to take their food out of the microwave and it would then go cold.* | *Make it beep when the cooking time is complete. Make it beep every minute after that until the door is opened.* |
| Auto-pilot on an aeroplane | *High winds might blow the plane off its course.* | *Have a warning for the pilot if the winds are too high so that they can switch to manual pilot.* |
| Guided missile | *Target may have moved.* | *Have a way of over-riding the system to re-direct or disarm it.* |

# 5.2

## End of Unit Activity: Photobooth (Suggested solution)

Your task is to create a detailed flowchart to show how a photo booth system would be controlled.

The basic steps are:

1. Person sits in the photo booth.
2. The booth is operated using a touch screen.
3. The person selects what type of photographs they want. This booth will print one large photograph or four small passport style photographs.
4. They insert payment. One large photo is cheaper than 4 passport-sized ones.
5. The photo booth takes the photograph or photographs.
6. After about 30 seconds the photographs are printed.

*Suggested solution below.*

*The solution shown is a L6 solution. L4 would include most of the steps but it may lack precision and efficiency. L5 should include all the steps but may not be efficient. The efficiency of this solution could be further improved by using a counter to repeat the photograph and wait command four times rather than writing them all out individually.*

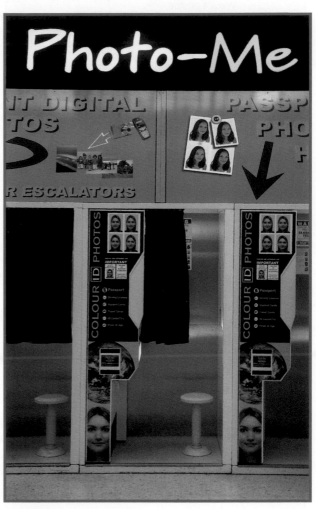

**Figure 1** A photo booth

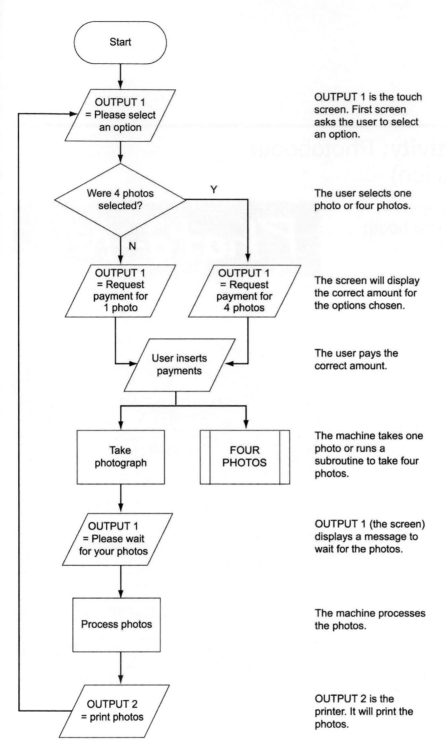

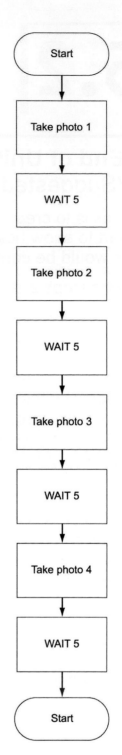

**Figure 2** Flowchart showing how to control a photo booth

**Figure 3** Flowchart showing how multiple photos are taken

**Written Task:** Writing efficient instructions (Suggested answers)

Your task is to re-write the instructions below so that they are more efficient. Your answers should be drawn as a flowchart.

1 These instructions make a microwave beep 3 times when it has finished cooking.

Beep on
Wait 1 second
Beep off
Wait 1 second
Beep on
Wait 1 second
Beep off
Wait 1 second
Beep on
Wait 1 second
Beep off
Wait 1 second

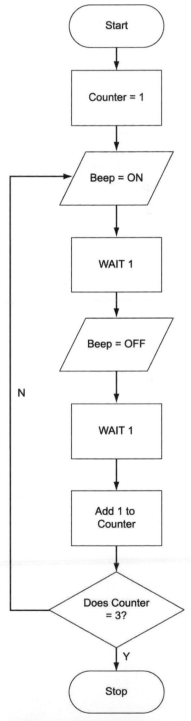

**Figure 1** Making a microwave flowchart more efficient

1 of 3

**2** These instructions take 4 photographs in a passport photo booth.

Message on the screen reads: Photo will be taken in 5 seconds

Wait 5

Take photo

Message on the screen reads: Photo will be taken in 5 seconds

Wait 5

Take photo

Message on the screen reads: Photo will be taken in 5 seconds

Wait 5

Take photo

Message on the screen reads: Photo will be taken in 5 seconds

Wait 5

Take photo

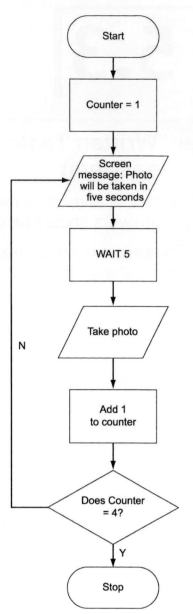

**Figure 2** Taking multiple photos

**3** Create a flowchart for a password system on a computer. If the user puts the wrong password in three times, they are locked out of the system.

MAIN

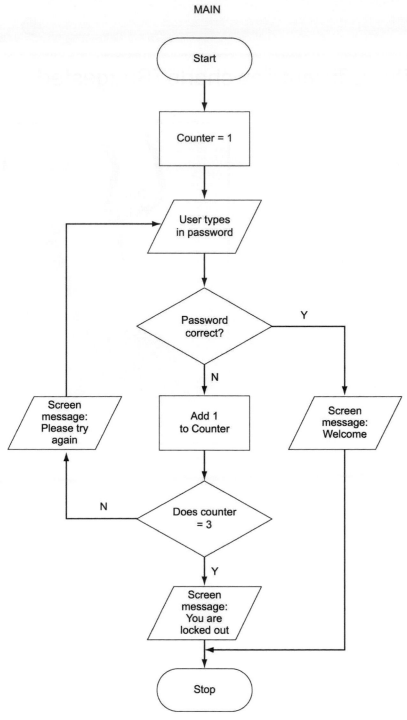

**Figure 3** Locking a computer system

# 5.3

## End of Unit Activity: Efficient flowcharts (Suggested solution)

Your task is to create a flowchart to control this exercise bike.

This is how it works:

1  The user uses the control panel to select how long they want to cycle for.
2  At the end of the time, the machine beeps three times.
3  The display shows them how far they have travelled.

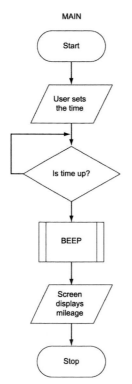

**Figure 2** Flowchart showing how to control an exercise bike

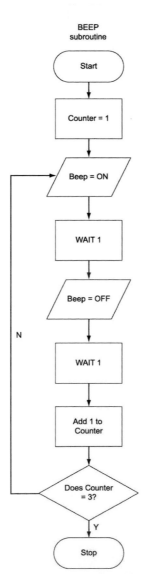

**Figure 1** An exercise bike

**Figure 3** How the bike measures time

# 5.3

### End of Unit Activity: Efficient flowcharts (Suggested solution)

Your task is to create a flowchart to control this exercise bike.

This is how it works:

1 The user uses the control panel to select how long they want to cycle for.
2 They choose between two options: 'Free Ride' or 'Real Ride'. Free Ride means that they just pedal for the chosen time. Real Ride is more like a real bike ride. The machine adjusts the resistance on the pedals every 30 seconds to make it harder to pedal (as if you were going up hill).
3 At the end of the time, the machine beeps three times.
4 The display shows them how far they have travelled.

**Figure 1** An exercise bike

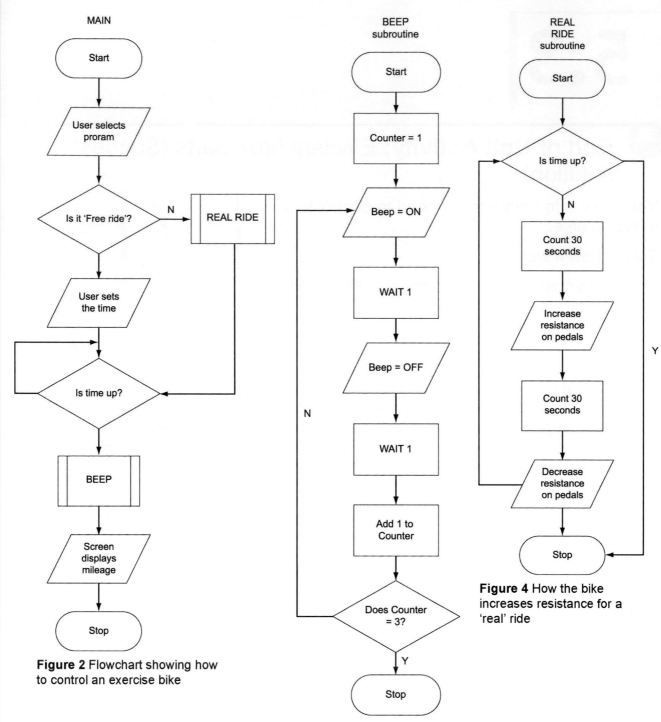

MAIN

Start

User selects proram

Is it 'Free ride'? — N → REAL RIDE

User sets the time

Is time up?

BEEP

Screen displays mileage

Stop

**Figure 2** Flowchart showing how to control an exercise bike

BEEP subroutine

Start

Counter = 1

Beep = ON

WAIT 1

Beep = OFF

WAIT 1

Add 1 to Counter

Does Counter = 3?

N

Y

Stop

**Figure 3** How the bike measures time

REAL RIDE subroutine

Start

Is time up?

N

Count 30 seconds

Increase resistance on pedals

Count 30 seconds

Decrease resistance on pedals

Y

Stop

**Figure 4** How the bike increases resistance for a 'real' ride

# 5.4

 **Written Task:** Monitoring and control systems (Suggested answers)

Your task is to complete the table below. The first one has been done for you.

| Monitoring and control system | What is being monitored? | What does the control system do? |
|---|---|---|
| Speed cameras | Vehicle speed | The system is able to calculate whether the vehicle is travelling too fast. If it is, it will take a digital photograph of the car, including the number plate. The date and time and the speed that the car is travelling at are all recorded. |
| Supermarket freezer | *Temperature* | *The system takes regular readings of the temperature. If it is too cold, it will stop refrigerating. If it is not cold enough it will start refrigerating.* |
| Security camera | *Movement* | *Some systems only start recording if they sense movement. Other systems are monitored by humans. Others are on all the time. Some systems can track movement; those controlled by humans use a joystick.* |
| Car park entry system | *Button being pressed.* *Number of vehicles entering and exiting.* | *The barrier will go up when the button is pressed. The number of cars entering and exiting is recorded. If the car park is full, it will not let any more cars in until someone leaves.* |
| Central heating system | *Temperature* | *The system takes regular readings of the temperature. If it is too cold, it will turn the heating on. If it is too hot it will turn the heating off.* |

# 5

## End of Module Assignment: Controlling a tollbooth (Suggested solution)

Your task is to create a flowchart to control the tollbooths on a toll road.

This is how they work:

1 The red light is on and the barrier is down.
2 The driver drives up to the barrier and pays the attendant.
3 The attendant presses a button and the barrier goes up.
4 The green light comes on.
5 After 10 seconds the barrier goes down again.
6 The red light comes on.

**Figure 1** Tollbooths

*Typical L4 response shown below. L5 would have a little more precision e.g. the green light is switched off before the red light is put back on again.*

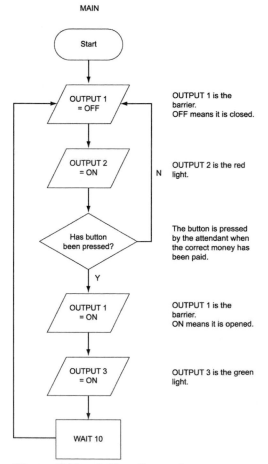

**Figure 2** How tollbooths work

# End of Module Assignment: Controlling a tollbooth (Suggested solution)

Your task is to create a flowchart to control the tollbooths on a toll road.

This is how they work:

1 The red light is on and the barrier is down.
2 The driver drives up to the barrier and pays the attendant.
3 The attendant presses a button and the barrier goes up.
4 The green light comes on.
5 After 10 seconds the barrier goes down again.
6 The red light comes on.

**Figure 1** Tollbooths

7 Drivers who use the toll road every day can buy a smart card which they put inside their windscreen (next to the tax disc). If they have one of these, it will be read automatically and the barrier will open if it is valid.

*L5/6 response shown below. L5 will have this level of precision but may not have used the subroutine. L6 will use a subroutine.*

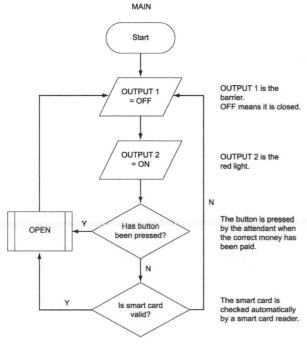

**Figure 2** How tollbooths work

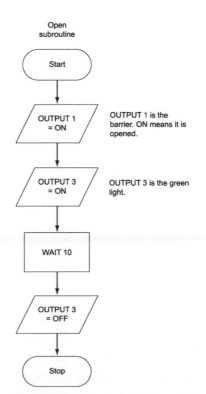

**Figure 3** Subroutine for controlling the barrier

# 6

 **Starter Activity** (Suggested answers)

You should view the Module 6 Case Study before you try these activities.

**1** What impact does ICT have on our social lives?

> *We use ICT to communicate with other people through mail, instant messaging, website forums, texting, mobile phones.*
> *We use ICT for entertainment, e.g. music, films, games, socialising.*
> *We can meet new people online, e.g. in forums, on social networking sites (like MySpace and Bebo).*
> *Pupils may widen the discussion to include ways in which ICT and ICT devices make our lives easier and more convenient.*

**2** What impact does ICT have on employment in this country?

> *Pupils should realise that ICT creates many jobs but that it might also mean that some people lose their jobs, or have to retrain. They should also realise that the pattern of work might change, for example, more people work from home.*
> *Examples of jobs created include: web designers, computer technicians, call-centre operatives.*
> *Examples of jobs that might be lost or changed: bank clerks, shop workers, factory workers.*

**3** In what ways has ICT improved our lives?

> *Some ICT makes our lives easier or more convenient, e.g. mobile phones, DVD recorders.*
> *Some ICT makes our lives safer, e.g. smoke and burglar alarms, automatic pilot systems on aeroplanes.*
> *Pupils may refer back to the improvement in social lives and the use of ICT for entertainment and leisure.*

**4** In what way has ICT had a negative effect on our lives?

> *We may have become over-reliant on ICT, which could be a problem if it fails.*
> *Some people have lost their jobs or had to retrain because of the effect that ICT has on jobs.*
> *Some people spend too long on computers, which can have a negative impact on their health and social skills.*
> *ICT may contribute to global warming.*
> *Some ICT devices don't last very long and then have to be thrown away as they can't be recycled.*
> *There is a lot of undesirable material and activity that takes place, particularly over the Internet.*

 © Hodder Education 2008

**5** What laws might people break when they are using ICT?

> *Pupils may not know the names of the laws at this stage but they should be aware of:*
>> *Copyright and what it applies to*
>> *Problems with copying and pasting directly from the Internet*
>> *Hacking, spreading viruses, and phishing are other issues that pupils may know about*
>> *Issues relating to the Data Protection Act.*

**6** Why might some people in the UK not be able to get access to ICT?

> *They may not have enough money to be able to buy computers and ICT devices.*
> *They may not have the necessary education, particularly if they are older and did not have ICT lessons at school.*
> *There may be religious reasons why they don't use ICT.*

**7** Why might people in other countries not use ICT as much as it is used in the UK?

> *They may not have enough money and the money they do have is spent on more essential items.*
> *They may not have a reliable power supply or computers.*
> *They may not have the necessary education.*

DL DYNAMIC LEARNING © Hodder Education 2008

# 6.1

 **Written Task:** Misuse of data (Suggested answers)

Read the article about identity theft (on the pupil activity worksheet) and then answer the questions below.

1 What is identity (ID) theft? *When someone steals your personal information, such as your name, address and financial details. They then pretend to be you.*

2 How could you personally be affected if someone stole your ID? *Pupils may not be badly affected as they don't tend to have bank accounts. However, ID fraudsters could still set up bank accounts and buy things online in their names.*

3 How could your parents/guardians be affected if someone stole their ID? *Parents are more likely to be affected as they have bank accounts. Parents may find that they have large credit card bills to pay, or get charged for things they have not bought. The fraudster could take out a loan in their parents' name, which the parents then have to pay off.*

4 What organisations store personal data about you and what do they use this data for?

*School – stores personal details so they can contact home if necessary; store data on exam results to track progress; store data on discipline record.*
*Doctor – stores medical data, which is useful for diagnosing problems and prescribing drugs; records dates of injections, etc. so they know you are up to date.*
*Dentist – stores medical data relating to your teeth, which they use to make sure you get the right treatment.*
*Pupils may identify other organisations such as clubs, ISPs or websites that they may be registered with.*

5 Are you worried about identity theft? Explain your answer.

*There could be a range of responses here. Some pupils may not see the relevance yet as they are not financially independent. Many may see it as a problem for when they are older. Some may have family or friends who have been affected by it and may relate personal experiences.*

# 6.1

 **End of Unit Activity:** Keeping personal data safe
(Suggested answers)

Your personal data are at risk all the time. Your personal details could be stolen, or there could be mistakes in the information people store about you.

Your task is to complete the table below explaining what risks there are to you or members of your family and what you can do about it.

The first one has been done for you.

| Risk | What can I do about it |
|---|---|
| Spyware software could install itself on your computer when you are online. | Be careful which sites you visit, as spyware often comes from illegal download sites or games sites. Use spyware removal software on a regular basis. Install a firewall. |
| *Someone might send an email pretending to be from the bank asking for bank account details. This is called phishing.* | *Never give your bank account details out in an email. Banks will never ask for your bank account details using email.* *Use anti-phishing software.* |
| *If you give your details to a company, they might pass them on to other companies.* | *Be careful which websites you put your personal details into. For example, if you are registering for an email address, you don't have to put your full address in.* *Most businesses have a tick box that you can tick so that they do not send your details to other companies. Make sure you tick this box.* |
| *An organisation might have incorrect information stored about you.* | *Ask to see the information that is stored. Ask the organisation to put it right if it is incorrect.* |
| *A virus could delete the personal information that you store on your own computer.* | *Use anti-virus software.* *Back up your files to a safe place, such as a CD, which you store away from the computer.* |
| *Someone might hack into your system and find information in your personal files.* | *Use a firewall to prevent hackers.* *Password-protect personal files.* |

# 6.2

 **Written Task:** Health and safety policy (Suggested answers)

Your task is to write a Health and Safety Policy for the use of the computers at your school. This policy is a document that explains the rules that you think everyone in the school should follow if they are to stay healthy and safe while using computers.

You should write something for each of these headings:

## 1 Avoiding accidents

*Pupils should include having appliances checked, not drinking near computers and not overloading electrical sockets. They should also include being careful about trailing cables.*

## 2 Avoiding strain injuries

*Pupils should include information on eyestrain, headaches, arm, hand, wrist or finger strain, shoulder and back strain.*

*The policy should include advice on how to avoid these strains including:*

> *Take regular breaks away from the computer.*
> *Adjust the position of the screen so that there is no glare.*
> *Set the brightness to reduce the amount of glare.*
> *Adjust your sitting position so that you are comfortable.*
> *Angle the keyboard rather than using it flat.*
> *Use foot and wrist rests.*
> *Make sure the room you are working in has the right heating and lighting and is not too noisy – not always easy when you are at school!*
> *Get rid of all the clutter around your computer so you have got room to work.*

## 3 Avoiding stress

*Pupils should explain situations that lead to stress. For example, having work deadlines, or being pressured by others.*

*Pupils should provide advice, including:*

> *Write out a plan (or list) of everything that needs doing.*
> *Take regular short breaks away from the computer.*
> *Show respect in the way you deal with other people, including when you are online.*

# 6.3

 **Written Task:** Plagiarism (Suggested answers)

**1** What is plagiarism?

*Copying someone else's work and pretending that you did the work yourself.*

**2** Where did you get your definition from – did you copy it straight from the Pupil's Book?

*Pupils should realise they need to put the explanation in their own words.*

**3** Why might someone object to having their work copied?

*Someone might spend a long time creating their work and they might object to someone else getting the credit for it if they did not do it.*

*Someone might make money out of what they have plagiarised. For example, if an author plagiarised someone else's story, they might make a lot of money by selling a book with the same story in it.*

*Plagiarism is basically stealing and many people see it as morally wrong to steal.*

**4** What is wrong with plagiarism?

*Some people think it is morally wrong because it is stealing.*
*The person who has stolen the work does not learn anything.*
*It could be illegal if the work that has been plagiarised is copyrighted.*
*The person who plagiarises can get themselves into lots of trouble. They could even be sued.*

**5** What can you do to make sure that you do not get accused of plagiarism?

*Clearly state where you got your information.*
*Don't copy and paste direct from the Internet.*
*Put information into your own words.*
*Use more than one source of information.*
*Get permission to use information supplied by other people.*

# 6.3

 ## End of Unit Activity: Copyright and you (Suggested answers)

**1** For each item in the table, explain where you get a legal copy and explain who owns the copyright. The first one has been done for you.

| Item | Where you can get it from legally? | Who owns the copyright? |
|---|---|---|
| Music track | Legal download sites such as iTunes. Buy the CD online or from a music shop. | Usually the person or group that wrote the track. |
| Music video | *Legal download sites.* *Buy the CD/DVD online or at a music store.* | *The copyright for the song would be owned by the songwriter. The copyright to the video will probably belong to the director of the video or the company that made the video.* |
| Film | *Legal download sites.* *Buy the DVD.* | *The film company, e.g. Disney.* |
| Software | *Download from the software company website.* *Buy the CD that contains the software online or from a computer shop.* | *The software company, e.g. Microsoft.* |
| Computer game | *Download from the game developer's website.* *Buy the CD that contains the game online or from a computer shop.* | *The game developer, e.g. Sony.* |
| Digital photograph | *Take the photograph yourself.* *Pay a photographer for the photograph.* *Download legally from the Internet either from a photographer's website or photograph library (like ClipArt).* | *The photographer.* |

**2** Why is copyright so important to writers, artists and musicians?

*These people make a living from the books, pictures or music that they sell. They are paid a royalty when someone buys their work. For example, every time a music CD is sold, some of the money goes to the band. Without copyright, these people would not get paid and would not be able to make a living.*

**3** Why do you think some software companies give their software away for free?

*Some companies give some of their software away for free as a way of encouraging you to buy some other software that they make. For example, they might give away a basic version and then you would have to pay to buy an enhanced version.*

*Some companies give software away for free because they believe that software should be free. For example, the Linux operating system is completely free. You can download this onto your computer and it means that you do not need Windows.*

**4** How would you feel if you found that someone had copied some work that you had done, and then claimed that it was theirs? Explain your answer.

*Most pupils are likely to feel aggrieved if someone sold their work on the basis that it is usually seen as being morally wrong to cheat or steal. Many pupils will simply feel it is unfair for people to get credit for things that they have not done.*

**5** If someone examined your computer, how could you prove that all the music, films, software and photographs were legal?

*In theory we should all have licences and receipts for everything that is on our computers. For example, we should keep the packaging and original CD/DVD when we buy software as this is the licence.*

*Many software companies now get you to register the software online, which proves that you have bought a legitimate copy of the software.*

*When we buy music or films on the Internet, we are sent a receipt and we should keep this as proof of purchase.*

# 6.4

## Written Task: ICT in developing countries (Suggested answers)

A developing country is one where the people are relatively poor, but where they want to become richer. For example, some countries in Africa fall into this category.

A developed country is one where the people are relatively rich. For example, the UK falls into this category.

**1** Why do you think that people in developing countries use ICT less than people in developed countries?

*They may not have the necessary power supply.*
*They may not have the computer equipment.*
*They spend the money they have on more essential items such as food and shelter.*
*They do not have the same access to education and may not have the skills to use ICT.*
*They will not use ICT for entertainment as much as in developed countries.*

**2** In what ways could ICT be used to help people in developing countries?

*They can use the Internet to find customers for their products all over the world.*
*They can use new technology to improve their education and health services.*
*They can develop new technology to produce the food and other products they need more efficiently.*

**3** What disadvantages might there be to using more ICT in developing countries?

*It might divert money away from more essential needs.*
*There might be cultural or religious objections to new technology, particularly the Internet.*
*It might affect employment, e.g. people might lose their jobs.*

India is what is known as a Newly Industrialised Country (NIC). ICT is widely used in India and they are becoming the best in the world in some areas of ICT. For example, lots of computer software is now written in India.

**4** Who benefits from having software written in India?

*Wages are lower in India, so the cost of making the software is lower. This means that software may become cheaper for us to buy.*
*There are high levels of programming skill in India, so software may have less bugs in it.*
*The programmers benefit as they get a job out of it and they will be relatively well-paid.*

 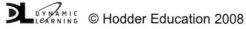

**5** Who is disadvantaged by having software written in India?

*Programmers in other countries will be disadvantaged as they may lose their jobs if the work is sent to India. Or they may have to work for less pay themselves.*

**6** Sometimes when you phone a UK bank or insurance company, the call is answered in a call centre in India. What are the advantages and disadvantages of this?

*Advantages:*
*The bank or insurance company has lower costs because wages are lower in India.*
*We may get cheaper banking or insurance as a result.*
*Indian workers get reasonably well-paid jobs out of it.*
*It brings money into India so it becomes a slightly richer country.*

*Disadvantages:*
*UK workers may lose their jobs if the work is done in India.*
*It takes money out of the UK so it becomes slightly poorer as a result.*
*There may be language problems.*

# 6.4

 ## End of Unit Activity: The impact of ICT (Suggested answers)

**1** In what ways does ICT benefit you personally?

*Pupils may draw examples from all areas of ICT including its use:*
> *To access information for educational purposes, for example on the Internet*
> *To increase efficiency, for example word-processing homework*
> *For leisure and entertainment*
> *To communicate with others*
> *To make life easier or improve the quality of life.*

**2** In what ways does ICT benefit society as a whole?

*Provides employment.*
*Provides access to information.*
*Improves services such as health, education, national security, air travel etc.*
*Provides entertainment.*

**3** What problems might be caused by the use of ICT?

*Over-reliance on computer technology could be a problem if it fails.*
*It can cause unemployment or change the nature of people's jobs.*
*It can make people unsociable or unfit, for example if they play computer games all the time.*
*There is a lot of undesirable material sent electronically.*

**4** Why might some people not be able to get access to ICT?

*They may be poor and cannot afford a computer.*
*They may not have the necessary skills and education to use ICT.*
*They may live in a developing country where they don't have electricity, computers or phone lines for the Internet.*
*They may be old and may never have had any training in ICT.*
*They may have disabilities such as impaired vision which mean that standard ICT equipment is not adequate.*
*They may have religious objections to the use of ICT.*

**5** What do you think should be done to help people get access to ICT?

*Government schemes to provide training and funding.*
*Computers and the Internet available through schools and libraries.*
*Training courses for anyone that wants them.*
*Charitable funding to developing countries so they can afford the equipment.*

# 7.2

The 'Choose and Book' system works using a database that stores details of patients, hospitals and appointments.

Your first task is to show how you could set up this database. Complete the table below showing:

1 What information (fields) you think needs to be collected

2 What data type each field should be

3 What validation checks could be added on each field.

*A suggested field list is shown here. Pupils may suggest other appropriate fields.*

| Field name | Data type | Validation |
|---|---|---|
| First Name | Text | Must be answered |
| Last Name | Text | Must be answered |
| Address | Text | Must be answered |
| Gender | List | Male or Female<br>Must be answered |
| Date of Birth | Date | Must be answered |
| Chosen hospital | List | Names of the hospitals<br>Must be answered |
| Hospital department | List | Names of the hospital departments<br>Must be answered |
| Date of appointment | Date | Must be after today's date<br>Must be answered |
| Time of appointment | Date/Time | Must be between 9:00am and 5:00pm<br>Must be answered |
| Name of Doctor | Text | Must be answered |

Your second task is to look at the 'X-ray appointments' database. This shows the bookings for x-rays over the last week.

Your task is to examine the database and answer these questions:

1 How many people used the 'Choose and Book' system last week? *99*

2 Which appointment times were most popular, morning or afternoon? *Afternoon*

3 Which hospital was the most popular? *Pickworth*

# 7.2

 **Practical Task:** GP database (Suggested answers)

The 'Choose and Book' system works using a database that stores details of patients, hospitals and appointments.

Your first task is to show how you could set up this database. Complete the table below showing how you would set it up.

*A suggested field list is shown here. Pupils may suggest other appropriate fields.*

| Field name | Data type | Validation |
|---|---|---|
| First Name | Text | Must be answered |
| Last Name | Text | Must be answered |
| Address | Text | Must be answered |
| Gender | List | Male or Female<br>Must be answered |
| Date of Birth | Date | Must be answered |
| Chosen hospital | List | Names of the hospitals<br>Must be answered |
| Hospital department | List | Names of the hospital departments<br>Must be answered |
| Date of appointment | Date | Must be after today's date<br>Must be answered |
| Time of appointment | Date/Time | Must be between 9:00am and 5:00pm<br>Must be answered |
| Name of Doctor | Text | Must be answered |

Your second task is to look at the 'X-ray appointments' database. This shows the bookings for x-rays over the last week.

One of the GPs wants to have a look at what appointments have been made over the last week. She wants to know:

1 How many people used the 'Choose and Book' system last week? *99*

2 Which appointment times were most popular, morning or afternoon? *Afternoon*

3 Which hospital was the most popular? *Pickworth*

Create a report for the GP that gives her the information she needs in a suitable format. *Pupils should produce the information perhaps in the form of a report. They may use tables or graphs to present the results.*

# 7.2

 **Practical Task:** GP database (Suggested answers)

The 'Choose and Book' system works using a database that stores details of patients, hospitals and appointments.

Your first task is to show how you could set up this database.

*A suggested field list is shown here. Pupils may suggest other appropriate fields.*

| Field name | Data type | Validation |
|---|---|---|
| First Name | Text | Must be answered |
| Last Name | Text | Must be answered |
| Address | Text | Must be answered |
| Gender | List | Male or Female<br>Must be answered |
| Date of Birth | Date | Must be answered |
| Chosen hospital | List | Names of the hospitals<br>Must be answered |
| Hospital department | List | Names of the hospital departments<br>Must be answered |
| Date of appointment | Date | Must be after today's date<br>Must be answered |
| Time of appointment | Date/Time | Must be between 9:00am and 5:00pm<br>Must be answered |
| Name of Doctor | Text | Must be answered |

Your second task is to look at the 'X-ray appointments' database. This shows the bookings for x-rays over the last week.

One of the GPs thinks that:

> Some hospitals are more popular than others
> Patients prefer morning appointments
> Patients prefer morning appointments after 10:30am

Use the database to test these two ideas and create a report for the GP that gives her the information she needs in a suitable format.

*Pupils may produce a report using graphs and tables.*
*They should carry out filters, queries or produce a graph to identify the number of people choosing each hospital.*

1 of 2

*The figures are:*

*Pickworth: 45*
*Queens: 14*
*Kings: 25*
*Strand: 15*

*Therefore, the first hypothesis is true – some hospitals are more popular than others.*

*They should then carry out filters or queries or produce a graph to test the second hypothesis. They will need to filter or query on the Morning/Afternoon field. The figures are:*

*Morning appointments: 59*
*Afternoon appointments: 40*

*Therefore, the second hypothesis is also true – people prefer morning appointments.*

*The final hypothesis will require a filter or query on the Morning/Afternoon field and the Appointment time field. The figures are:*

*Before 10:30am: 16*
*10:30am and after: 43*

*Therefore, the final hypothesis is also true – patients prefer appointments after 10:30 in the morning.*

DL DYNAMIC LEARNING © Hodder Education 2008

# 7.3

**Practical Task:** Hurricane model (Suggested answers)

The 'Hurricane Predictor' model can be used to predict whether a hurricane is likely to happen. It looks at three main causes of hurricanes: wind speed, ocean temperature and air temperature. You can type in what the readings are for each of these three as: HIGH, MEDIUM or LOW. For example, if the wind speed were high, you would set the reading to HIGH. It then looks at the three readings and works out how likely it is that there will be a hurricane. Your task is to look at the model and answer the questions. You will only need to change the cells in blue in column B.

1  What three factors does the model use to predict hurricanes?

   *Wind speed*
   *Ocean temperature*
   *Air temperature*

2  What is the risk of a hurricane with these settings? *LOW*

   Wind speed = HIGH
   Ocean temperature = LOW
   Air temperature = LOW

3  What is the risk of a hurricane with these settings? *HIGH*

   Wind speed = LOW
   Ocean temperature = HIGH
   Air temperature = HIGH

4  What is the risk of a hurricane with these settings? *HIGH*

   Wind speed = LOW
   Ocean temperature = HIGH
   Air temperature = MEDIUM

5  What is the highest the "Total hurricane rating can be"? *9*

6  What is the lowest the "Total hurricane rating can be"? *1*

7  What is the purpose of the cell colours used in cell C10? *Green is LOW, Orange is MEDIUM and Red is HIGH. Hotter colours indicate higher levels of danger.*

8  What effect does wind speed have on the risk of a hurricane? *The lower the wind speed, the more likely it is that there will be a hurricane.*

9  What effect does air temperature have on the risk of a hurricane? *The higher the air temperature, the more likely it is that there will be a hurricane.*

10  Explain what combination is most likely to cause a hurricane? *Low wind speeds, high air temperature and high ocean temperature.*

**DL** *DYNAMIC LEARNING* © Hodder Education 2008

# 7.3

 **Practical Task:** Hurricane model (Suggested answers)

The 'Hurricane Predictor' model can be used to predict whether a hurricane is likely to happen. It looks at three main causes of hurricanes: wind speed, ocean temperature and air temperature. You can type in what the readings are for each of these three as: HIGH, MEDIUM or LOW. For example, if the wind speed were high, you would set the reading to HIGH. It then looks at the three readings and works out how likely it is that there will be a hurricane. Your task is to look at the model and answer the questions. You will only need to change the cells in blue in column B.

1  What is the risk of a hurricane with these settings? *HIGH*

   Wind speed = LOW
   Ocean temeperature = HIGH
   Air temperature = MEDIUM

2  What is the highest the "Total hurricane rating can be"? *9*

3  What is the lowest the "Total hurricane rating can be"? *1*

4  What is the purpose of the cell colours used in cell C10? *Green is LOW, Orange is MEDIUM and Red is HIGH. Hotter colours indicate higher levels of danger.*

5  What effect does wind speed have on the risk of a hurricane? *The lower the wind speed, the more likely it is that there will be a hurricane.*

6  What effect does air temperature have on the risk of a hurricane? *The higher the air temperature, the more likely it is that there will be a hurricane.*

7  Explain what combination is most likely to cause a hurricane? *Low wind speeds, High air temperature and High ocean temperature.*

It has been discovered that atmospheric pressure is also a factor when predicting hurricanes.

Update the model to include atmospheric pressure with these settings:

LOW = 3
MEDIUM = 2
HIGH = 1

You will need to change the formula for the risk of hurricane to use the following settings:

Total hurricane rating <5 then Risk of hurricane = LOW
Total hurricane rating >5 and <9 then Risk of hurricane = MEDIUM
Total hurricane rating >=9 then Risk of hurricane = MEDIUM

1 of 2

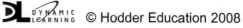 © Hodder Education 2008

*See the Hurricane model (L5-6 Solution) file.*
*Notice that a new row 7 has been added with the new variable.*
*The formula in cell C7 has been put in to make set the hurricane rating to 1, 2 or 3.*
*The formula in cell C11 has been updated because the rating is now out of 12*
*instead of 9 as it was with only three variables.*

**8** What is the risk of a hurricane with these settings? *HIGH*

Wind speed = LOW
Ocean temperature = HIGH
Air temperature = MEDIUM
Atmospheric pressure = LOW

**9** What is the risk of a hurricane with these settings? *MEDIUM*

Wind speed = HIGH
Ocean temperature = HIGH
Air temperature = LOW
Atmospheric pressure = LOW

**10** What is the risk of a hurricane with these settings? *LOW*

Wind speed = HIGH
Ocean temperature = LOW
Air temperature = LOW
Atmospheric pressure = HIGH

ICT InteraCT for KS3 2        DL DYNAMIC LEARNING © Hodder Education 2008

# 7.3

 **Practical Task:** Hurricane model (Suggested answers)

The 'Hurricane Predictor' model can be used to predict whether a hurricane is likely to happen. It looks at three main causes of hurricanes: wind speed, ocean temperature and air temperature. You can type in what the readings are for each of these three as: HIGH, MEDIUM or LOW.  It then looks at the three readings and works out how likely it is that there will be a hurricane. It has been discovered that atmospheric pressure is also a factor when predicting hurricanes.

**1** Explain what combination is most likely to cause a hurricane?

*Wind speed = LOW*
*Ocean temperature = HIGH*
*Air temperature = HIGH*

**2** Update the model to include atmospheric pressure with these settings:

LOW = 3
MEDIUM = 2
HIGH = 1

You will need to change the formula in for the Risk of hurricane to use the following settings:

Total hurricane rating <5 then Risk of hurricane  = LOW
Total hurricane rating >5 and <9 then Risk of hurricane  = MEDIUM
Total hurricane rating >=9 then Risk of hurricane  = MEDIUM

*See the Hurricane model (L5-6 Solution) file.*
*Notice that a new row 7 has been added with the new variable.*
*The formula in cell C7 has been put in to set the hurricane rating to 1, 2 or 3.*
*The formula in cell C11 has been updated because the rating is now out of 12 instead of 9 as it was with only three variables.*

**3** What is the risk of a hurricane with these settings? *HIGH*

Wind speed = LOW
Ocean temperature = HIGH
Air temperature = MEDIUM
Atmospheric pressure = LOW

**4** What is the risk of a hurricane with these settings? *MEDIUM*

Wind speed = HIGH
Ocean temperature = HIGH
Air temperature = LOW
Atmospheric pressure = LOW

**5** What is the risk of a hurricane with these settings? *LOW*

    Wind speed = HIGH
    Ocean temperature = LOW
    Air temperature = LOW
    Atmospheric pressure = HIGH

**6** Based on the research you did in Task 1, explain what changes you could make to the model to make it more realistic. If possible, make the necessary changes.

*Pupils should refer back to the research they did for Task 1. They might identify that the model is too simplistic and suggest changes such as:*

*Using more accurate readings rather than HIGH, MEDIUM and LOW.*
*Use real-life readings from sensors that are constantly updated.*
*Include more variables such as: wind direction, humidity, time of year.*

CT InteraCT for KS3 2